Pat Chen is one of the people I admire most. She is a veteran Christian leader whose vision is global and whose knowledge of God runs deep.

—JOHN DAWSON
FOUNDER, INTERNATIONAL RECONCILIATION COALITION

Pat Chen is a woman I hold in high esteem. Having served with her in leadership for many years, I have found her to be a woman of great integrity. Her heart for God has the capacity to draw those around her into greater intimacy with Him.

—JANE HANSEN
PRESIDENT AND CEO, AGLOW INTERNATIONAL

This modern-day Shulamite speaks to us as one who has come up from the wilderness, leaning upon her Beloved. She bids us to "rise up and come away," that we might know the One on whom she leans. This book is addressed to those who desire a deeper and more intimate walk with God.

—KELLY ALLEN
FRIEND AND INTERCESSOR
ANCHORAGE, ALASKA

Having lived in close quarters as Pat's husband for thirty-one years, I have been allowed a firsthand look at a Proverbs 31 woman. I have seen the Lord grow and mentor her in the most amazing ways in His sensitivity, wisdom and insight. I am truly a blessed man because of her love for me and her deep devotion for our Lord Jesus Christ. I am sure the Holy Spirit will help many through this book to become more intimate with Him.

—PETER H. C

Intimacy With the Beloved

A PRAYER JOURNEY
INTO THE DEPTHS
OF GOD'S PRESENCE

Pat Chen

CREATION
HOUSE

INTIMACY WITH THE BELOVED by Pat Chen
Published by Creation House
A division of Strang Communications Company
600 Rinehart Road
Lake Mary, Florida 32746
www.creationhouse.com
www.charismalife.com

Unless otherwise noted, all Scripture quotations are from the New American Standard Version of the Bible. Copyright © 1960, 1962, 1963, 1968, 1971, 1972, 1973, 1975, 1977 by The Lockman Foundation. Used by permission.

Scripture quotations marked NKJV are from the New King James Version of the Bible. Copyright © 1979, 1980, 1982 by Thomas Nelson, Inc., publishers. Used by permission.

Scripture quotations marked TLB are from The Living Bible. Copyright © 1971. Used by permission of Tyndale House Publishers, Inc., Wheaton, IL 60189. All rights reserved.

Scripture quotations marked KJV are from the King James Version of the Bible.

Library of Congress Catalog Card Number: 99-75216
International Standard Book Number: 0-88419-590-2

Definitions given in this book are taken from the following sources: *Webster's New Twentieth Century Dictionary* (William Collins Publisher, Inc., 1979) and *Strong's Exhaustive Concordance of the Bible* (Nashville, TN: Regal Publishers, Inc.).

0 1 2 3 4 5 6 VERSA 8 7 6 5 4 3 2 1
Printed in the United States of America

I dedicate this book to my Beloved, the Lord Jesus Christ—my heavenly Bridegroom.

In memory of my brother, Roderick, who had Down's Syndrome. Though he was blind and could not speak, he taught us how to love. Today he walks the streets of heaven completely healed.

In memory of Wanda, who was a true servant. To me, Wanda was an Enoch—who walked with God and she was not—for during worship God took her.

I *would like to thank:*

My husband, Peter, and my son, Kenon.
You are the two loves of my life.

My family, for all of your love,
prayers and encouragement.

Cecilia, for your countless hours of support
and help with this book.

All my intercessors, for your strong
and faithful prayers.

CONTENTS

PREFACE

Y FIRST CALLING is to be prostrate before the Lord Jesus Christ in prayer and worship. I am His, and He is mine.

Recently I sought the Lord while staying at a retreat lodge, which was situated at the foot of a mountain in California. As I shared my concerns about my prayer ministry with the Lord, He spoke to my heart: "You don't have a prayer ministry. I am your ministry." So what can I say? Jesus is my ministry!

Through my life of ministry to Him, I have discovered that no matter who you are, you can have a close relationship with the Lord. This wonderful communion with God is not for the select few—it's for whosoever will. It's not just for the super-spiritual giants we promote. It's for everybody. I want people to experience and know the passionate love that Jesus has for them.

As you read through the pages of this book, my earnest prayer is that you will be ushered into the healing presence of

His love, and that you will discover a new place of personal encounter with Him. May the Holy Spirit lead you on your own personal journey of intimacy with the Beloved.

—PAT CHEN

INTRODUCTION

ID YOU KNOW that a rapture will take place before the rapture of the church of Jesus Christ into glory? The first rapture will not be a catching away of bodies, but an enrapturing of our hearts with fiery love for Jesus, our Beloved. Before we, His bride, hear the last trump, our hearts will be swept up into the heavenlies, caught away in a holy love affair with God. We will have such a longing for the Bridegroom that we will call out for His return from the depths of our souls. We will cry, "Maranatha!"–which means, "Our Lord, come!"

The rapture of our hearts, the catching away of our desires and affections, is a holy outpouring of love from an expectant bride awaiting her Bridegroom's appearance. This is the divine romance. This is intimacy with the Beloved. He is your refreshing drink; so come, and be satisfied with Him.

And the Spirit and the bride say, "Come!" And let him

who hears say, "Come!" And let him who thirsts come. Whoever desires, let him take the water of life freely.

—REVELATION 22:17, NKJV

SECTION 1

THE
PRESENCE

May he kiss me with
the kisses of his mouth!
For your love is better
than wine.

—SONG OF SOLOMON 1:2

1

Visitations of
the Holy Spirit

*A*s WE JOURNEY to a place of deeper intimacy with God, we will have times of special visitations by the Holy Spirit. How grateful I am that the Lord extends His grace to us this way. These times of precious fellowship are filled with wonder and awe as the heart of God is revealed. These holy touches of His Spirit are a foretaste of glory—a glimpse of the heavenly ecstasy that awaits us beyond the veil of this life. These moments of spiritual envelopment are like being kissed by the love of God.

THE KISSES OF GOD'S PRESENCE

HOLY VISITATIONS ARE not experiences we can make happen. Jesus doesn't come to visit us at just any time, but He does come when it's appropriate for Him—and not always when it's convenient for us.

I experienced a visitation of the Holy Spirit during a season of prayer in a rustic cabin situated at Lord's Land Retreat in California. This simple structure, tucked away in the Mendocino Woods, was transformed into a holy altar of God's presence.

The one-room prayer cabin was equipped with a wood-burning stove, cold-water faucet, two chairs and a cot. As I entered, I looked out the giant window and was taken aback by the display of beauty. I felt surrounded by the God of all creation.

I climbed up to a loft, which contained one small window and a skylight. Through the skylight I watched clouds pass across the bright blue sky. Looking from the small window in front of me, I delighted in the view of tall redwood trees and dense woods. Thanksgiving and praise to God flowed out of my spirit for the glory of His workmanship.

POUR OUT YOUR HEART

MY TIME AT the cabin was limited, so I began to pray earnestly. I whispered, "Lord, I feel that I scarcely know You, but I want to know You much better. The more I know You, the more I realize how very little I truly know You. I want to see You. I want to sense Your presence. I want to be like You, and I want to be with You." My heart yearned for more of Jesus.

Suddenly God's presence poured over me like liquid love. I sensed, in a very tangible way, the nature of His unconditional love for me. At that moment, the Lord was everything to me—I cared about nothing else. He flooded my soul with His indescribable glory.

As the Holy Spirit moved upon me, my heart began to break with a feeling of desperation for God. Utterly broken, I expressed to the Lord what I felt deep within. Often I have experienced the deep stirrings that make me who I am. But I seldom speak of them. On this occasion, I poured out my innermost thoughts and feelings to God. I had climbed up to the loft and touched heaven's glory. I knew my life would not be the same after this, for I was being changed from glory to glory.

Each of us is unique, and we experience different kinds of encounters with God. Some individuals call these experiences "power encounters," because God's presence is so overpowering. In these encounters we discover the nature and personality of the Holy Spirit. His love has many different moods and expressions. As the Spirit of God pours Himself in and over us, we may remain aware of the objects around us. Nonetheless, it seems as if nothing and no one else is around but Jesus.

GIVE HIM FIRST PLACE

IN GOD'S POWERFUL presence it's never an effort to yield our minds, our time and our plans to the Lord. There is no contest with Him; He always has preeminence. We must always give Him first place. He is *Adonai,* the Sovereign One.

When His presence rushed in upon me, I hadn't been seeking a particular experience. My prayer was, "I just want to know You, Lord." Is this your prayer as well? When God's presence overwhelmed me, He was simply responding to my heart's cry. There was nothing for me to think about or do. There was no preparation—just a brief, heartfelt whisper of a prayer.

I could not say, "God, wait. Just hold it off for a few minutes and let me climb down from this loft, because I need to go back up the hill to get something." That was never a consideration. At that moment of visitation, nothing else mattered but God. I had entered into eternity, and time meant nothing. I was in a safe place, with a safe person—Jesus, the Lover of my soul. No thinking was necessary on my part, because the Lord had already been thinking about this encounter. It was a part of His plan. And God has a plan and purpose for special encounters with you, too. God drew my heart by the gentle tugging of the Holy Spirit. He wooed me. He wants to woo you.

DEVELOP A SENSITIVITY TO HIS PRESENCE

WHEN I FIRST walked into the prayer cabin, I sensed the presence of the Lord there. When we practice His presence daily and spend much time in prayer, we become sensitive to Him. He gives us an ability to discern His nearness.

When I sense the slightest nudge of the Holy Spirit, my spiritual ears perk up. I start listening, and my spirit-man opens up to receive Him. I try constantly to be receptive to the Lord. It's not a difficult thing. He gives us the ability as we practice being in His presence often.

Entering into God's presence becomes less and less of an effort as you yield your spirit to Him. It's like keeping your spiritual antenna up, always waiting for a signal from above. Sometimes, no matter what, it may seem like an effort to press through the many distractions of the flesh and mind. We are human, fallible and finite, and sometimes we're dull in spirit. But God will help us.

DON'T TURN AWAY FROM HIS URGING

AT TIMES IT requires no effort to enter into God's presence. For me, these are seasons when I have a deep, Spirit-driven hunger and thirst for the things of God. These are times of intense spiritual desire for Him, when I don't want to take any chances of missing Him. At such times I respond to the slightest whisper of the Spirit's call.

You see, if I miss such a moment, if I fail to respond to the

Holy Spirit's prompting, the opportunity for that particular spiritual experience may never come again. Something wonderful may have been lost forever. This is one of the most important lessons I've learned over the years about waiting upon the Lord and receiving from His Spirit.

Often people come to me and share how they shrugged off or pushed away the presence of the Lord, and later they were sorry. Pride got in the way and caused them to miss something that God had for them. They let circumstances and worldly pressures dictate how they should use their time. The Lord called them into a wonderful experience, but they felt compelled to get up and get busy, or they had to do a few more little chores before waiting for Him on their knees.

If you get a nudging from the Lord that He's drawing you to prayer, never shrug it off—never turn away. Never say, "Not now, Lord." Allow Him, at that very moment, to minister to you or touch you or speak to you—whatever it is He desires to do. This is how you develop a greater sensitivity to His voice. Eventually you will learn how to wait upon Him as you go about your activities.

Is this "power encounter" a learned experience? No. But what is learned is yielding. Every time you yield yourself to God, you give more of yourself to Him—more of your heart, your plans, your desires, your hopes and your dreams.

The Lord surprised me that day in the prayer cabin in the Mendocino Woods. The presence of God poured into the room and flowed over me. His wonderful touch overwhelmed me. It was too precious an experience, too sacred, to stop or say no. Our God is a God of surprises. Will you accept His surprise package for you?

A TASTE OF HEAVEN

WHEN I FIRST began to experience this intimate relationship

with the Lord, at times God gave me a glimpse of Himself. He gave me a taste of heaven.

Some people claim to have spiritual experiences, but the source of their experiences is their imaginations, not God. You can always judge a person's experience by the Word of God, by his character and by the fruit of his relationship with God. True spiritual encounters increase your desire to know God and His Word. Tasting heaven makes you heavenly. Your character is transformed. You can know if a person's touch from heaven is genuine. Every time we behold the face of Jesus Christ by encountering the Holy Spirit, we are transformed. We become more like Him. Each touch of heaven transforms us into the likeness of God's Son.

> But we all, with unveiled face beholding as in a mirror the glory of the Lord, are being transformed into the same image from glory to glory, just as from the Lord, the Spirit.
>
> —2 CORINTHIANS 3:18

GIVE HIM CONTROL

THE HOLY SPIRIT within us is big, and He is able. How big is God? He has total dominion over whatever He chooses, and He has ownership. He is the light and life within us already. And He desires to see His life revealed through our lives so that others may be touched by His wonderful love.

When we yield to His presence, His anointing increases upon us and flows through us. It's much easier to resist the Holy Spirit than to submit to Him. Our flesh demands control. When we yield to His Spirit we lay down that control and resist the demands of the flesh.

Temperance, or self-control, is listed among the fruit of the Spirit. (See Galatians 5:22–23.) It's a wonderful quality. In the natural, we fear anything that makes us feel out of control. But as we yield the control of our earthly lives and bodies to the Holy Spirit, we find that He is a much better manager of our time and lives than we are.

THE SECRET PLACE OF THE MOST HIGH

WHEN I ENTERED into the prayer cabin, the Spirit of the Lord was already there. We can actually come into a room and find that the Lord is there waiting for us. But there's a place in the Spirit that goes beyond what I experienced at the prayer cabin. What I'm describing has nothing to do with entering a room. That is what happened next.

We can come into His presence in prayer and find that His presence becomes the very place in which we're praying. It's as if you're suddenly transported from your prayer closet to the spiritual realm. You're no longer on earth but praying in the holy of holies. That's what happened to me. No longer was I in a cabin. I was in Him. In such moments you experience Him. When you're in this kind of communion with Him, you become one with your Lord. He is the room—He is everything! Nothing exists outside of Him.

This is more than an encounter with the power of God; it is being intimately aware of the personality of God. It's the Holy Spirit revealing Jesus Christ to you. (See John 14:16–31.) His presence is not just a feeling. He is a Person. You can get to know His personality and His character of pure love, kindness, tenderness and acceptance. When God visits, you sense what He feels toward you: complete, unconditional love. You experience a sense of fulfillment that cannot be described. In your heart you talk to Him, and He responds by talking to you. Sometimes you hear words, but other times are marked only by an awareness of what He's feeling or thinking.

At the prayer cabin, God's unmistakable presence revealed

7

His deep love for me. The joy of such moments is inexpressible.

> In Thy presence is fulness of joy; in Thy right hand there
> are pleasures forever.
>
> —PSALM 16:11

PRESSING DEEPLY INTO HIS PRESENCE

I LEARNED HOW to yield to the presence of God by pressing into Him, that is, by being deliberate about my pursuit. When I sensed His presence, I humbled myself enough to admit that I wanted the Lord desperately. I longed for His nearness. I wanted whatever He had for me, and so I pressed in.

The Bible encourages, "Draw near to God and He will draw near to you" (James 4:8). The Holy Spirit draws us into God's presence through an intense desire birthed in our hearts by the Holy Spirit. As I read the Word of God, it draws me nearer to Him.

Such desire for God comes only from God. Ask Him to draw you to Himself. Ask Him from a pure heart to renew the flame of desire within you. The Bible tells us that godly hunger comes from above. We cannot manufacture it. Ask Him to fill your waiting heart with desire for Him. Ask your heavenly Bridegroom to draw you into His secret place.

> Draw me after you and let us run together!
>
> —SONG OF SOLOMON 1:4

THE WELL OF HIS PRESENCE

AS I SAT in a rocking chair in front of the wood-burning stove, a deer walked up to the cabin. I continued to rock and pray in my heavenly language, and a cloud of God's presence descended upon me once more. This time He gave me a picture of a deep well that He was digging within me and within the hearts of other believers.

The Holy Spirit speaks and teaches us in so many ways. Sometimes God gives us dreams and visions. The Spirit of God came upon me and began to teach me about the well of His presence. It is this well from which mankind longs to drink. It is the well of salvation and wholeness deep within the believer's heart that only God can dig. He alone fills that well with living water and causes it to overflow. The Lord is giving the body of Christ a greater capacity to receive from Him and, therefore, an ability to give to others more freely. Our world is needier than ever, and we will be used by God to meet those needs in the coming years as never before.

> "Behold, God is my salvation. I will trust and not be afraid. For the LORD GOD is my strength and song, and He has become my salvation." Therefore you will joyously draw water from the springs of salvation.
>
> —ISAIAH 12:2–3

This well of God restores and brings rest within. It provides you with immeasurable satisfaction. Once you discover this well, you will keep coming back for more. Nothing else can satisfy and quench your thirst like a drink from this well of fresh water.

The well of living water will take away your thirst for the world and the things of this life. Until they taste for themselves, others will never fully understand the goodness of the Lord. The Word of God says, "O taste and see that the LORD is good; how blessed is the man who takes refuge in Him!" (Ps. 34:8).

A believer will never truly know the riches of God's goodness until he drinks from the well of His pleasures. This well refreshes with every taste. The rivers of God rush from the deep streams within, from tributaries and recesses that others will never understand.

> There is a river whose streams make glad the city of God.
>
> —PSALM 46:4

HITTING ROCKS

WHEN THE ANOINTING of God overshadowed me that morning, in my mind's eye I saw a deep stream and a well. I noticed that many streams came from the river, running over and under the ground. In the natural realm, some streams are on the surface of the ground, and others are down underneath in layers of the earth. If you go down far enough, you'll eventually hit rock.

That's precisely what I saw concerning the body of Christ: layers of rock, blocking the flow of water. Then the Spirit of God flowed downward through layers of rock, making a way free. Until we experience this freedom, we must constantly pray for revival in the body of Christ.

Why do some of our encounters with the Lord seem to be deeper than others? We have many layers in our beings, and sometimes we hit a layer of rock that needs to be removed in order to get down to the next level of water.

We may encounter hindrances to prayer that reside in the realm of our souls. These layers of rock must be removed. Perhaps the rock is unforgiveness or stubbornness or rebellion. These hard places in our hearts resist the Holy Spirit and hinder us from moving deeper into a rich prayer life.

As we press into God, the Holy Spirit reveals these rocks so they can be removed. Once a layer of rock has been removed, our hearts become softer and more yielded to the Spirit. Free of these hindrances, we often experience a release of the anointing into our lives and ministries. Repentance helps remove the rocks of hindrance every time.

When you pass through a layer of rock and get to the next level, something wonderful happens. You begin to drink from His storehouse of pleasures. His love refreshes you and fills your every longing. You realize what you've been searching for all your life. His loving presence brings wholeness, health and a sense of well-being that no food, drug, medicine, person, material good or worldly pleasure can ever produce.

This kind of release in prayer will leave you breathless.

AS THE DEER LONGS FOR THE WATER

As I LOOKED out the prayer cabin, remembering the deer that came up to my window earlier, it occurred to me that this is the kind of relationship described in Psalm 42. Our hearts are not only like a gentle deer, but they are also like a desperate deer that has been hunted by an enemy. Our hearts long for a refreshing drink from a brook of living water.

> As the deer pants for the water brooks, so my soul pants for Thee, O God.
>
> —PSALM 42:1

Part of the thrill of an intimate relationship with the Almighty is the waiting and the pursuing—it's in the panting after Him. Sometimes that panting is desperate, when it seems you can't go on until you are refreshed with God's water. Psalm 42 has been the single most important scripture in fulfilling my life's calling and message.

God alone can remove the stones, the rocks of sin and the secrets we keep—even from ourselves. All of us keep secrets from other people, but there are secrets about us that God keeps from us. There are things about myself, things I don't realize and can't see, that He keeps from me to protect me. He knows what's within me, and He knows what needs to be removed from my heart. He knows what gifts and callings need to be stirred. He knows all that is within my heart—even the treasures of His Spirit, the gifts He has placed there.

God comes to us in moments of visitation because He enjoys us and wants us to enjoy Him. Fellowship with Jesus is a mutual delight; it's never just one-sided. This sweet fellowship is made even sweeter by knowing it also gives Him pleasure. It is not just our hearts that long for God. His heart longs for us as well! He enjoys us.

WAITING FOR HIS PRESENCE

WE DON'T KNOW how to wait. The Lord calls; He beckons us to come and be with Him, but we don't know how to wait for Him. So often we give up too soon—we get discouraged. But it is worth the wait.

Instead of waiting, we try to fulfill our desires and longings with substitutes. But what is required of us is simply to wait—sometimes for days. Set aside time for God alone. These are times of remaining quiet, of meditating upon His Word, of sometimes worshiping and always praising Him. The discipline of waiting is something many of us know little about.

When His presence comes into our prayer closets, He often comes with power, love and passion. His Spirit enters like a mighty, rushing wind—a great big surprise package wrapped with a big bow.

When you experience Him in this way, you may cry aloud, "You, Lord, are the joy of my soul's desire! You fill my heart with laughter and song. My heart is filled with love for You, O God. Put back together all the broken pieces of my life. Blow away my insecurities with the breath of Your Spirit. Wash me in Your presence. I want nothing more than to be with You in Your glorious presence."

At other times, He may come with utter silence and still-ness, and you may not be able to move or speak a word. Such a visitation of God's presence is fearsome.

Our God is truly a God of "suddenlies." He will come upon your waiting heart in an instant. You may also experience long seasons during which you feel nothing, see nothing and hear nothing as you wait for His presence. It doesn't matter. He is there watching your every move and listening to your every thought. He knows, and He is there with you.

Are you willing to wait silently, expectantly, for Him? Will you pay this price for intimacy with your heavenly Bride-groom? Ask Him to teach you to wait upon Him.

A GARDEN LOCKED

ONLY GOD CAN dig this wellspring, and only God can fill it. If you are a believer, deep within your heart is a well of God's Spirit. Much has been placed within you that only God knows about and understands: gifts of the Spirit, anointings, long-ings, visions, plans and purposes of God. Others can drink from your wellspring as the life of God flows out of you through your words, actions and deeds.

Not only can the treasures of God's Spirit deep within you refresh others, but God Himself desires to be refreshed by your love. This is the communion He desires.

> A garden locked is my sister, my bride. A rock garden
> locked, a spring sealed up.
> —SONG OF SOLOMON 4:12

Just as God alone can dig this well, only He can unlock the garden of our hearts. That's what happened to me as I sat there in the rocking chair. Something was unlocked. When it became unlocked, I received revelation knowledge from His Word and a fresh understanding of His desire for me. This is the washing of the water of the Word. (See Ephesians 5:26.)

Many different things get in the way and lock up this garden of our hearts. Only the Lord Jesus, the Lover of our souls, can come and unlock the garden within us! He is the One who holds the key, but we must give Him permission to enter and unlock the passageways inside.

Some have said that the key is on the inside, and we are responsible for opening the door. However, He has the combination. He knows the formula that will take that last turn. He knows what will unlock the door and release His presence within us. He does it all.

We may try to make God come to us in the same ways He has in the past. But we soon discover that we cannot. I've tried, and it doesn't work. We can never expect that the same types of holy visitations will be repeated in our lives when and how we want them. We just have to wait for Him. What happened in the prayer cabin was not planned. God ordains when He will visit, and each encounter is unique and orchestrated by Him.

BLESSING GOD

> Awake, O north wind, and come, wind of the south; make my garden breathe out fragrance, let its spices be wafted abroad. May my beloved come into his garden and eat its choice fruits!
> —SONG OF SOLOMON 4:16

May the Lord Jesus linger here in the garden of my heart, in the spring of my desire, and delight Himself with my devotion. As His presence rests upon my aching heart, the fragrance of the Holy Spirit releases a sweet, heavenly aroma.

Many times we linger in His presence, enjoying the nearness of God. But never forget that He longs for our fellowship as well. We receive a greater blessing when our first desire is that God be blessed. Seek to discover what pleases Him.

What is it that fills His desire? We please Him by obeying His Word, for obedience is better than sacrifice. We please Him by sharing what we have with others. We also please Him by being alone with Him in prayer when He's not asking us to come, and worshiping Him when we're not seeking His blessings. Come before Him in abandonment and adoration, with a burning, passionate submission. May He be satisfied with our choice fruit, the fruit of the Spirit and of our love.

The greatest satisfaction we will ever know is in our inner man. In the natural, we seek only to satisfy ourselves. But when two are involved, there's a mutual delight.

Do you enter into God's presence with a longing for Him only? I encourage you to come into His presence at this very moment, seeking nothing more than to love Him, to worship His wonderful name and to delight in Him.

I AM MY BELOVED'S, AND HE IS MINE

LOVERS SPEAK WITH their eyes. We can feast upon the Lord as He feasts upon us. There is mutual delight in one another. Words are expressed that never have to be spoken between lovers.

> I am my beloved's and my beloved is mine, he who pastures his flock among the lilies.... Turn your eyes away from me, for they have confused me; your hair is like a flock of goats that have descended from Gilead.
> —SONG OF SOLOMON 6:3, 5

I use the words *real, genuine* and *vulnerable* when I teach others how to experience the depths of God's presence, because what will be revealed to you as you enter into His presence is both very human and very spiritual. This intimate relationship with the Lord puts you in a vulnerable place. You may be able to keep up your guard with man, but never with God. (See Hebrews 4:13.)

Vulnerable means "unprotected, unguarded, unshielded, accessible, assailable, defenseless." In the Lord's presence, our hearts are uncovered, and our souls are exposed. We become subject to Him because we experience surrender—a complete submission of everything we are. Giving total control to God puts you in a very vulnerable place.

THE PRAYERS OF IMPORTUNITY

THE PRAYER OF importunity is found in Luke 11. It has a lot to do with waiting upon God:

> And He said to them, "Suppose one of you has a friend, and shall go to him at midnight, and say to him, 'Friend, lend me three loaves; for a friend of mine has come to me from a journey, and I have nothing to set before him'; and from inside he answers and say, 'Do not bother me; the door has already been shut and my children and I are in bed; I cannot get up and give you anything.' I tell you, even though he will not get up and give him anything because he is his friend, yet because of his persistence he will get up and give him as much as he needs."
>
> —LUKE 11:5

This is the prayer of importunity: keep going, keep asking. It is persistent, prevailing prayer. I learned this as I waited upon God, seeking His presence for hours at a time as I pursued Him.

> And I say to you, ask, and it shall be given to you; seek, and you shall find; knock, and it shall be opened to you. For everyone who asks, receives; and he who seeks, finds; and to him who knocks, it will be opened. Now suppose one of you fathers is asked by his son for a fish; he will not give him a snake instead of a fish, will he? Or if he is asked for an egg, he will not give him a scorpion, will he? If you then, being evil, know how to give good gifts to your children, how much more will your heavenly Father give the Holy Spirit to those who ask Him?
> —LUKE 11:9

God wouldn't give you a snake if you asked for a fish, and if you asked for an egg, He wouldn't give you a scorpion. We are carnal and yet know how to give good gifts. How much better and kinder is our Father in heaven. He will delight you with His response when you ask Him for more of His Spirit.

Ask God for more of Himself, seek Him for a deeper walk in the Spirit and use the prayer of importunity with faith, knowing that He is a good God who desires to respond and give you all you need.

OUTWARD EXPRESSIONS

WHEN THE HOLY Spirit comes to reveal Jesus, some people shake, and some quake. God's transforming love is powerful, and spiritual power can affect you physically. Some whose experiences are always peaceful may disagree. But we are all unique. The power and presence of God ignites some individuals with a flame of Pentecostal revival, as has been recorded throughout history.

In days gone by, many of those who took part in great outpourings of the Holy Spirit quaked and cried out, not only in repentance, but also in fiery love and worship. Others were impassioned by God in deep wells of silence.

We seldom experience such things today in the body of Christ, even though the signs of renewal are flickering around the world. Don't be afraid of manifestations of the Spirit's power. Remember that God has created us all as unique beings. The physical expressions of God's power can be as unique as the individuals He touches. Never discount the validity of another's experience just because it's different from your own. Instead, choose to be awed at our Creator's diversity. Never judge your experience by another's, or another's experience by your own. Let God be God.

These experiences are between God and an individual; they are not for us to judge by our own preferences. We judge them by the Word of God, the fruit of the Spirit and spiritual discernment. (See 1 John 4.)

DISCERNMENT

TRUST REQUIRES YEARS of spending time waiting on God. When I first began to experience God's presence, I questioned the Lord often. "God, please don't let me go off the deep end," I would say.

It's been almost twenty-five years since I first experienced God's presence, and I haven't gone off and joined a cult. I haven't done any strange things. When you have a real experience with God, you want nothing but what is real.

Some people are afraid to experience the Lord's presence because they fear the wiles of the enemy. We need to be guarded. We must not allow ourselves to be given over to other spirits. Make sure your experience is of God, not of the devil or the flesh. At the same time, we have to trust God. Believe in God, and trust Him to protect you. Come to a place of abandonment where you so trust in the Lord that you can yield to Him without fear. Luke 11:13 says that He will give good gifts to us—not evil. The precious blood of Jesus Christ covers us and protects us as we submit to Him and commit our way to His care.

Always ask yourself what is the fruit of an experience. You can tell when an experience is not of God by what it produces in your life. What does it make you do? How does it make you feel? How does it make you think? Act? What are the results of the experience? Every encounter should bring you closer to the Person of Jesus Christ. Each visitation should draw you into worshiping Him.

A genuine experience with the Holy Spirit will draw you into the Word of God. It will never be contrary to His character and nature. How do you know? The Scripture says to *test the spirits* and see if they are of God (1 John 4:1). I did a lot of testing as God started bringing me into new depths of His presence, and I still test the spirits. I was always cautious when the presence of God started to come down upon me, even when I received my prayer language—tongues. I thought, *Is this God?* You must test the spirits.

God will always confirm the legitimacy of your experience by showing it to you in the Bible. As He increases your understanding of His Spirit, He will also increase your understanding of His Word. You see, the Bible says that the Word and the Spirit must always agree. Your encounter with the Holy Spirit will always reveal Jesus, and it will always make you want more of Jesus. It will always draw you back into who He is. It's a humbling experience—it never leads to spiritual pride.

BALANCE

As the Spirit of God draws you deeper into fellowship with Himself, you will also open your heart to Him in increasing measure. That's part of being vulnerable. At times it feels like risky business. This self-serving nature we've inherited must die in the light of God's holy presence.

Never look for an experience for the sake of an experience. If you seek spiritual experiences, then you may get what you're seeking—but they may not be from God. Instead, seek the Lord. Some people don't need or want experiences, and they don't seek them. I would never attempt to change their point of view. But if someone is hungry to experience God in a deeper way, I believe that desire is placed there by God.

Spiritual hunger does not reside in us naturally. Anyone whose heart's desire is to know God in a deeper way is not in the flesh. The carnal person doesn't desire to touch God or to know and experience Him. (See 1 Corinthians 2:11–16.) The natural man desires only the things of this world. A hunger for the deeper things of God is a gift of the Holy Spirit. This hunger is God drawing us closer, allowing us a foretaste of glory.

It's a very good thing to want to know God and experience Him. However, we must maintain a balance. There may be times when we must go about our daily lives and serve Him without any sense of His presence at all. Our Christian walk must always be built upon the character of Christ in our lives and upon a firm foundation of the Word. Our lives cannot be built upon experiences, for experiences will come and go. But the Bible tells us that the Word of God will endure forever. When our lives are founded upon the rock of God's Word, no storm of life will ever move us. (See Matthew 7:24–25.)

Nonetheless, our faith doesn't have to be devoid of spiritual experiences. The Word of God records the lives of many people who encountered Jesus Christ supernaturally. Don't be afraid of spiritual experiences—they are treasures that will change your life. Just maintain a balance with God's help and grace. It's always good to have a seasoned counselor, a prayer leader or a pastor with whom to share your experiences for confirmation. Some have forfeited a life-changing experience because they didn't understand God's balance for them.

FEARFULLY AND WONDERFULLY MADE

EVERY ONE OF us is fearfully and wonderfully made. We are unique; therefore we have various ways of expressing our love to God. When we come into the presence of a holy God, we gain a fresh revelation of *who we are* because of the revelation of *who He is.* As we humble ourselves, we respond to God in ways that may be different from our usual ways because we shed our self-consciousness. When you come into the presence of a holy God, when you touch the hem of His garment, when you experience His glory, you cannot always remain composed.

OVERWHELMED BY HIS PRESENCE

AS I PRAYED in my private retreat, His presence over-whelmed me, and I could hardly take a breath. I felt as if I had been in a cocoon, and then in a moment He sur-rounded me with His presence. I abandoned myself to Him, and He bathed me in His love.

What happens when you come into His presence? It is incomprehensible! An encounter with the Lord makes you dif-ferent; it transforms you. He takes up ownership, and you become His.

Years ago, I would lie prostrate before the Lord for hours,

praying or waiting, sometimes not uttering a word. Sometimes I experienced hours of groaning in the Spirit. I felt as if I had entered heaven, yet I didn't leave the body. I know that those experiences were of God because of the fruit they've borne in my life.

EXPERIENCES IN GOD'S PRESENCE

WHEN I WAS first slain in the Spirit, I didn't understand what was happening. I went to a Pentecostal service and sat in the back pew because I was afraid of the display of spiritual power I saw there. When I went forward in this tiny church, I found myself prostrate on the floor. I wondered if the evangelist had pushed me down. I had never seen a move of the Spirit before. Here I was on the floor, in my first intoxication in the Spirit. I started laughing. Soon I was crying. God was healing years of hurt in me and revealing His supernatural power to me. My legs turned to rubber; I stood up and tried to walk, but I couldn't. I acted like a drunk person. When I went home and told my husband about it, he also asked if the evangelist had pushed me down.

I found the Lord's touch to be such a delightful experience that I wanted to receive it again. So I tried to figure out ways to make it happen again. It doesn't work that way. A couple of times I went down "under the power" of my own volition, trying to duplicate that first experience. When I tried to make it happen, it was not the same thing, because the flesh was involved. The Lord told me to wait for the real experience. So I started praying and asking the Lord to help me receive whatever He wanted in the way He wanted me to receive it. I asked God to forgive me for wanting the artificial. When we choose to wait upon God for what is real, we may not get to experience the supernatural all the time or as much as we would like. But it's worth the wait.

AN EXPECTANT HEART

YOU NEVER KNOW when He's going to come, but always have an expectant heart. When you wait, and He comes, it's the most rewarding experience. Our God is an awesome God. You are also aware that you did nothing to cause it to happen. It is completely from heaven.

Don't limit God by telling Him how to come or what to do or how to do it. As you mature, it's not "Give me, give me; I want, I want." Instead, it's "What do You want, Lord? How can I minister to You? What makes You happy? Are You pleased with me? How can I bless someone else with what You've given me?"

What kind of beloved
is your beloved, O most
beautiful among women?
What kind of beloved is
your beloved, that thus
you adjure us?

—SONG OF SOLOMON 5:9

2

Who Is the Beloved, and What Is Intimacy?

HE SONG OF Solomon poses the question: "What kind of beloved is your beloved?" In other words, who is your Beloved? Why and how is your Beloved better than any other? Why is He so wonderful? Why is He so different? How well do you know Him? How long have you known Him? What does He look like to you? Does He satisfy your soul? Does He meet your needs? Do you know what pleases Him and displeases Him? Do you please Him and bless His heart?

HE IS LIFE ITSELF

THE SCRIPTURES ARE very clear about who the Beloved is. (See John 1:1–5.) He is the One who was from the beginning of time. He is very present now, and He always will be. He is God, and He is *my* God. When He speaks, life breaks forth, and something is created out of nothing. When He speaks, all heaven comes to attention, for He is the Word. He is life itself. He is the light of the world, and His light overpowers and dispels all darkness.

When you come to know Him, you become one with Him. You become a prophetic voice crying in the wilderness: "A voice is calling, 'Clear the way for the LORD in the wilderness; make smooth in the desert a highway for our God'" (Isa. 40:3). You take an active part in preparing the way for the second coming of your Bridegroom. You become the bride, one who is intimate with your beloved Lord. Just as John the Baptist went before Christ at His first coming, you are now sent from God as the Beloved's witness wherever you go—with your life, your love, your words, your actions.

HE IS THE BAPTIZER

"JOHN ANSWERED THEM saying, 'I baptize in water, but among you stands One whom you do not know'" (John 1:26). The Pharisees didn't know Him, and those who are Pharisees today don't know Him either. "It is He who comes after me, the thong of whose sandal I am not worthy to untie" (v. 27). The lovers of Jesus are like John, who yielded to the will of God even when others rejected him. They are humble before the Lord Jesus, realizing they are not worthy even to loose His sandal.

Like John the Baptist, the lovers of Jesus know Him intimately, recognize Him immediately and proclaim Him boldly to the world. He's always first in everything they think and do.

Who is my Beloved, and what is He like? My Beloved baptizes me in His Holy Spirit. The Holy Spirit descended upon my Beloved as a dove out of heaven and remained upon Him until He left this earth. (See Matthew 3:16.) When Jesus left He promised not to leave us comfortless. He desired to be with us through the presence of the Holy

Spirit. He was not satisfied until He could be in us. My Beloved desires to commune with me through the power and presence of the Holy Spirit.

HE IS THE HEALER

WHO IS MY Beloved? He is a man of sorrows, sacrifice and grief. "Who has believed our message? And to whom has the arm of the LORD been revealed?" (Isa. 53:1). His flesh was ripped open until He was unrecognizable. Just as the beauty within Him could not be seen with the natural eye, the relationship we have with Him is not a natural one, but spiritual. The cross was horrible and yet beautiful, and He experienced a passionate love there. He's One whom I have rejected, but He has never rejected me.

My Beloved is *Jehovah Rapha,* the God who heals. He's my healer because He was willing to endure the scourging for my sake. My Beloved did not open His mouth to defend Himself. He is pure, honest and true. He can be trusted, for He is truth—He never lies.

He is my burden bearer. He bore the heavy weight of my sin on the cross. He bore my sickness and death to satisfy the good pleasure of the Father. He experienced deep intercession for my transgressions (Isa. 53:12). Therefore, He identified Himself with the transgressors. He knew no sin Himself, but He experienced sin on the cross to pay the cost of my salvation and healing.

HE IS THE WHOLLY DESIRABLE ONE

SONG OF SOLOMON 5:10 says, "My beloved is dazzling and ruddy, outstanding among ten thousand." He is more brilliant and powerful than the sun. Although His greatness is beyond my ability to fathom, He sees me as an individual.

When I'm in a crowd of thousands, He knows I'm there; He treats me as if I'm the only one who exists. Everyone is precious to Him.

"His mouth is full of sweetness. And he is wholly desirable. This is my beloved and this is my friend, O daughters of Jerusalem" (v. 16). He is a friend of sinners and my companion as well. He is my light, my salvation, my defense and my refuge. He is the One who encourages me and encompasses me. He is the One in whom I trust, for I do not trust in my own flesh. I have confidence in Him; I am secure in Him. He covers me, and He will lift me up and set me on a firm foundation.

What kind of Beloved do you have? Isaiah 46:5 says, "To whom would you liken Me, and make Me equal and compare Me, that we should be alike?" Who is my Beloved? He has no equal, and none can compare with Him. There is no one better than Him.

He will establish His purposes and accomplish all His good pleasures in my life. He who has begun a good work in me shall complete it. He will be faithful to me throughout my life, through the good times and bad, through my ups and downs.

Some husbands love their wives when they're young and beautiful but reject them when their youthfulness fades. But the Word of God says, "Even to your old age, I shall be the same, and even to your graying years I shall bear you! I have done it, and I shall carry you; and I shall bear you, and I shall deliver you" (Isa. 46:4). This is my Beloved. My Beloved stays with me even in old age when my hair turns gray. As I become more seasoned, He becomes more sweet. He won't leave me. He won't divorce me. When my face becomes wrinkled with age, He will still be faithful. My Beloved is the same, yesterday, today and forever. He is forever mine.

HE IS THE HEAVENLY BRIDEGROOM

WHO IS MY Beloved, and what kind of Beloved is He? He is a heavenly Bridegroom who is waiting the time of marriage with His church. "Let us rejoice and be glad and give the glory to Him, for the marriage of the Lamb has come and His bride has made herself ready" (Rev. 19:7). My Beloved is waiting for the time when we, His bride, will have made herself ready. At present we are being clothed with righteousness by walking in the character of Christ. The Holy Spirit prompts His bride, the church, to do acts of kindness to those who don't know Christ. This is one of the ways in which we prepare ourselves for the coming of the Bridegroom.

Sometimes it seems a lot easier to be kind to unsaved people than to those in the church. The Lord wants us to reach beyond the church but not to forget those sitting next to us on the pews each Sunday.

HE IS THE VICTOR

MY BELOVED HAS many names and descriptions. He is coming again on a white horse. When He does, He will have the final victory. My Beloved is King of kings and Lord of lords. He will judge everyone according to His deeds. He is the only One who can open the Book of Life. He will have the final say-so.

My Beloved will wash away every tear. There will be no more death, mourning or pain, for I shall live with Him in His dwelling place forever (Rev. 7:16–17). My Beloved makes all things new (Rev. 21:5). My Beloved is the Alpha and the Omega, the beginning and the end (Rev. 22:13).

HE IS THE COMING ONE

THE BRIDE OF Christ says, "Come, Lord Jesus." My Beloved is

One who says, "Yes, I am coming quickly." My Beloved speaks whatever the Father speaks, and He is inspired only by the Father. During the time of great temptation, He only said, "It is written..." (Matt. 4:4). Jesus, my Beloved, did whatever He saw the Father do and said whatever He heard the Father say. He never did anything contrary to the Father's will.

My Beloved is so beautiful to me that sometimes I feel like Paul, who said:

> For to me, to live is Christ, and to die is gain. But if I am to live on in the flesh, this will mean fruitful labor for me; and I do not know which to choose. But I am hard-pressed from both directions, having the desire to depart and be with Christ, for that is very much better; yet to remain on in the flesh is more necessary for your sake.
>
> —PHILIPPIANS 1:21–24

Paul faced a dilemma that everyone who becomes intimately acquainted with the Lord faces. He desired to go home to be with Him—not to escape the cares of this world, but because he wanted to see the Lord. While we wait to meet Him face to face, it's important to fulfill His purposes for our lives here on earth. As we do, we experience a sweet union and communion in the presence of our Beloved. He is sensitive to every intimate detail of our relationship.

His anointing dwells within us and is manifested through us. As we walk in fellowship with Him each day, what we have believed by faith will be realized by experience. Our experience is reinforced by the Word of God. Christ exists, and He is in our midst every day by the power of His Holy Spirit. God is real. He is tangible, and He can be touched, felt and recognized with unmistakable consistency.

WHAT IS INTIMACY?

INTIMACY IS A relationship with another that flows from a depth of knowledge and understanding that is shared by no one but the two individuals. Intimacy always requires making choices and taking risks. Intimacy reveals the real you that most people do not see. We all are complex beings, and most people never know us completely—except our Lord.

> For the crooked man is an abomination to the LORD;
> but He is *intimate* with the upright.
> —PROVERBS 3:32, EMPHASIS ADDED

Webster's Dictionary defines *intimate* as "closely acquainted or associated; very familiar; as an intimate friend." Intimacy involves disclosure, which means revealing the real you—your innermost self, your hidden thoughts, feelings and emotions.

Who we really are will surface at times and affect our relationships for good or bad—and even cause misunderstandings—but not so with God. He knows and understands everything about us, for He made us. He formed us in our mother's womb. He had us on His mind from the beginning of time.

Fear has no place in intimacy, for we must choose to trust completely to yield who we are to Him. We can trust in our Lord; He will never leave us or forsake us. Faith is required to believe we are accepted in the Beloved and will not be rejected, regardless of what we've done in the past. We choose to believe that we are accepted solely based upon His love for us.

INTIMACY REQUIRES HONESTY

THE ONLY REQUIREMENT for intimacy with God is that you be yourself. Pretense has no place in a truly intimate relationship. Intimacy leads you to receive and then to respond openly, without any expectation of being paid back.

True intimacy with God gives you the assurance that you owe no one anything but to love Him freely. When you understand the richness of a mutually intimate relationship, its worth is held so high that there's no hesitancy in giving back. Once you receive, you want to give back more and more. You can't outgive God, and it is more blessed to give than to receive.

Competition is out of the question in intimacy. Your delight is to bring joy and fulfillment to God and others. Your greatest satisfaction is to know that God is pleased with you, that your life is given to Him and that you have become a gift to others.

INTIMACY PRODUCES BIRTHING

THE LORD USES the natural things of this world to teach us about the spiritual realm. Just as intimacy with an earthly spouse births new life in the natural, intimacy with the heavenly Bridegroom births new life in the Spirit. As we come to know Jesus Christ in more intimate ways, fresh vision, insight, revelation, ministry gifts, power and anointing will be birthed in our lives. An anointing of power will descend upon our lives, touching those around us. Souls will be saved, people will be healed and the light of God will shine with greater brightness in all we say and do.

We can glean spiritual lessons from the miracle of conception. According to medical experts, *barrenness,* or the inability to conceive a child, is sometimes caused by an individual's behavior. One cause is pelvic infections from sexually transmitted diseases due to promiscuity. As a result, some women have blocked fallopian tubes that obstruct ovulation.

Similarly, an infection of sin or idolatry can prevent Christians from conceiving souls for the kingdom of God. When a person is spiritually promiscuous, he has no direction, no vision and no focus because of having too many partners. Our God is a jealous God. He will share us with no one. We are called to be totally His, a people of His possession. We are to have no other gods before Him.

> As for Ephraim, their glory will fly away like a bird—no birth, no pregnancy, and no conception!
> —Hosea 9:11

This scripture speaks of the spiritual barrenness that results from spiritual promiscuity or idolatry. As Christians we should expect to birth the life of God into the earth as a great harvest of souls. But when we flirt with other gods of materialism, rebellion and pride, we become barren, and our harvest is lost.

BIRTHING REQUIRES POWER, PASSENGER, PASSAGE AND POSITION

EXODUS 1:15–17 SPEAKS about the importance of midwives in the day of Moses. If not for them and their fear of God, Moses would have died during childbirth.

My grandmothers and some of my other relatives were midwives. A midwife helped bring me into the world. And just as my mother had help from a midwife to bring me forth, all creation groans for intercessors who will function as spiritual midwives to help others bring forth God's vision.

During childbirth, midwives rely upon these key principles: *power, passenger, passage* and *position*. If a woman cannot give birth, at least one of these four principles is out of alignment.

Problems can occur in the spiritual birthing process as well. Whether God has called His church to birth new souls into the kingdom or to bring forth a vision or purpose, obstructions can arise. A problem with natural childbirth may be caused by inadequate contractions or the lack of *power* to bring forth. With a lack of *power,* the body cannot push out the baby.

Just as many women lose strength at the end of their labor, many Christians lose heart and lack *power* right before the fulfillment of God's promise. What is wrought in secret spiritually will make a big difference in the open later for the kingdom of God. The church may lack power against the wiles of the devil. But we have hope for whatever lack we have in the Person of our Lord Jesus Christ. The Bible says, "Power belongs to God" (Ps. 62:11).

Another reason for failed childbirth may be due to the *passenger*—that is, the baby. When the mother is overdue, the infant is sometimes too large for her body to deliver. Fear can cause her not to relax enough to allow her to go into labor at the proper time.

The vision, or the spiritual *passenger,* may be too great for a small group of believers to bring forth without joining hands with others.

A third birthing problem occurs during *passage* when the mother's pelvis is too small.

So too in spiritual childbirth, fear may come upon believers with a vision, causing them to delay too long. This relates to *passage* in the natural realm. And this is why unity is so important—we must encourage one another in the process of bringing forth God's plan.

The fourth principle, *position,* is also critical. A baby poised in the wrong position can stop the birthing process.

The baby's head must be tucked down so that the smallest diameter of the head comes out first, with the chin on its chest. If the baby holds its head in an odd position, problems can result.

The *position* in spiritual childbirth may also be incorrect. Believers involved in birthing God's purpose may have moved from where they need to be through unbelief or deception. Because believers are not in their proper places, God's purposes are thwarted on earth. We need to be in the right place, at the right time, to bring about revival and the purposes of God.

God promises that His people, referred to as *Zion,* will give birth to the plans, visions and purposes He has given them, because He will help them. He promises to watch over the birthing process of the body of Christ to the delivery of His purposes. We will have fruit from our intimate walk with Christ, and our fruit will be healthy and will multiply.

> Before she travailed, she brought forth; before her pain came, she gave birth to a boy. Who has heard such a thing? Who has seen such things? Can a land be born in one day? Can a nation be brought forth all at once? As soon as Zion travailed, she also brought forth her sons. "Shall I bring to the point of birth, and not give delivery?" says the LORD. "Or shall I who gives delivery shut the womb?" says your God.
>
> —ISAIAH 66:7–9

INTIMACY REQUIRES TRANSPARENCY BEFORE THE LORD

IN THE PRESENCE of the Lord our masks are removed. The person we are on the inside is not always the person others see outwardly. We have learned to speak, think and act in ways that are acceptable to others. But when the Lord reveals Himself, if you receive Him as He is, the real you becomes exposed. The inner person hidden even to yourself is revealed—rough and unpolished.

The inner man is a complex person of many secrets, longings, motives and intentions. Who and what we are is not exposed to us all at once—even with God. Jesus reveals our inner man during precious encounters with Him. This is why I can express myself to the Lord in ways that I cannot to others. When I'm surrounded by the presence of God I discover who I am because I'm responding to who He is. He is truth, the Spirit of truth. I cannot hide from the truth of who I am in His presence.

Approaching the Lord in a nonsuperficial way is total nakedness of your soul. Transparency is required for total abandonment to God. We are imperfect human flesh with the perfect Holy Spirit of God living and moving inside of us. This fact astounds me. When you experience the depth of His presence, you respond to who He is. This is not a learned response; it is a revelation of the Lord revealing who you are. Each time I get a glimpse of who He is, I see more of who I am. My image is reflected off His brilliant light of truth, and in the midst of that I am still accepted in the Beloved. When you come face to face with the Lord, you become like Adam and Eve in the garden—naked before the Lord and unashamed.

WHO IS THE BELOVED, AND WHAT IS INTIMACY?

WHO IS YOUR Beloved? He is the One who invites you to discover a depth of relationship you never dreamed existed. What is intimacy? It is secure, settled and secret. It is that place of relationship, knowledge and love of Jesus.

Your heavenly Bridegroom invites you to know Him intimately. In that place of intimacy, a stirring will be birthed in your heart. From your raptured heart will flow the passion and life of God into the earth—birthing new souls, dreams, visions and the will and plans of God.

Your heavenly Bridegroom is tenderly knocking at the door of your heart, calling you to come into a deeper experience with Him. Will you answer His call to intimacy? Will you invite your Beloved to come in?

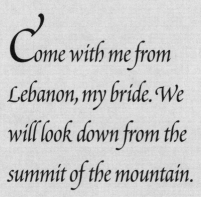

Come with me from Lebanon, my bride. We will look down from the summit of the mountain.

—SONG OF SOLOMON 4:8, TLB

3

A Bride Willing to
Pay the Price of Intimacy

EVERY BRIDE PROCLAIMS a commitment to her bridegroom alone—forsaking all others. This forsaking is the cost of the union and all that it promises. With the pledge of commitment comes the knowledge that she is accepting her husband for life—in wealth or poverty, power or weakness, fame or obscurity, health or sickness. But a bride never makes her pledge with these things in mind. Her pledge of devotion is always motivated by love. So shall it be at the wedding supper of the Lamb.

The Hebrew people look to God as their husband. Marriage is a more costly commitment than most of us realize until several years of hard experience are under our belt. As believers we must keep in our spirits the scripture that says: "For your husband is your Maker, whose name is the LORD of hosts; and your Redeemer is the Holy One of Israel, who is called the God of all the earth" (Isa. 54:5). With that knowledge operating in our spirits, our marriages have a better chance. No man or woman can meet your every dream or need. When God is your first love, you have a greater ability to love and give of yourself to your natural spouse. That way, your expectations are centered on God instead of on your mate.

Are you that bride who is willing to forsake all and pay the price for intimacy with Jesus Christ? The price He paid for you was very great. The cost to His bride is to give all, in loving devotion, to follow Him wherever He leads.

A BRIDE WILLING TO FOLLOW IN PASSION

Who has believed our message? And to whom has the arm of the LORD been revealed? For He grew up before Him like a tender shoot, and like a root out of parched ground; He has no stately form or majesty that we should look upon Him, nor appearance that we should be attracted to Him. He was despised and forsaken of men, a man of sorrows, and acquainted with grief; and like one from whom men hide their face, He was despised, and we did not esteem Him.

—ISAIAH 53:1–3

When Jesus hung on the cross, many spat on Him and mocked Him. They hated Him with a force born of the devil's own hatred. But it was Jesus' overwhelming love for the Father that incited the rage of His enemies. Jesus burned with this fiery passion to the point that He gave His life for us all. The forces of evil hated Him because He gave of Himself with a love that was pure, selfless and willing to suffer. This love was His passion.

The word *passion* is also defined as "ecstasy, delight, bliss, an expression of great joy, feeling, emotion, rapture, vehemence, zeal, affection, love, tender emotion, anger, fury, ardor, burning fire, flame or burn."[1] In *Webster's Dictionary* the word *passion* is also described as "to endure, to suffer" and originally, "suffering or agony, as of a martyr." At the crucifixion, those who stood off to the sides of the cross mocked Jesus. They hated His passion. They hated His love for all mankind. The bride says, "For God so loved the world, that He gave His only begotten Son, that whoever believes in Him should not perish, but have eternal life" (John 3:16). They hated His outward expression of love for us. He died to save us from our sins so we could have a relationship with the Father and be in heaven with Him. Because mankind is so selfish and self-centered, God's enemies could not endure that kind of love—love that is selfless and sacrificial.

"All of us like sheep have gone astray, each of us has turned to his own way; but the LORD has caused the iniquity of us all to fall on Him" (Isa. 53:6). Like most people, I sometimes think about what is good and comfortable for me. This is the mind-set of the flesh, the world and the enemy. But the expectant bride of Christ is willing to endure the same passion of the cross that He endured to save her.

WILLING TO SURRENDER AT
THE COST OF PERSECUTION

THOSE WHO GIVE themselves completely to Christ are often despised, mocked and looked upon as weird. The crowd demands that we prove who He is in us. They told Jesus to prove who He was. The world demands that we be just like everybody else. If we are not, they think something is wrong with us. We are constantly challenged to be like the crowd and to prove ourselves. But we don't have to prove anything. Jesus has already proven who He is on the cross. We must battle against those same mocking spirits that Jesus battled on the cross. The evil spirits are intruders into our private lives with

Christ. Our passion for Jesus is despised by the enemy. He hates our passion, and he hates us.

WILLING TO REJECT PEOPLE PLEASING

SOME PEOPLE WILL be jealous because of our passion and relationship with Jesus. Many will despise us because they want what they see in us but are not willing to pay the price to obtain it. So they will call out, "Crucify, crucify Him!" (Luke 23:21). If we are people pleasers, we cannot have God's best. If we must receive acceptance from others to fulfill our souls, even those in the body of Christ, we will not have the best that comes only from Him.

Ask for God's forgiveness and cleansing from old habits that put you in a place of receiving second best and becoming men pleasers. When challenged with this compromise, Peter and the other disciples withstood it. Peter and the apostles said, "We must obey God rather than men" (Acts 5:29). These compromises are the little foxes that spoil the vineyard of our love (Song of Sol. 2:15). Little habits and patterns of ungodly thinking spoil godly men and women. They are more insidious than the bigger things we've conquered. We want to have a certain image before people instead of a right image before the Lord. But to find true intimacy with God, we must deny ourselves, take up our cross and follow Him (Matt. 16:24).

WILLING TO SUBMIT TO
TOTAL DEVOTION AND ABANDONMENT

GOD'S PEOPLE WANT to glorify Him and bring Him great pleasure. Ask God to remove any blockages that hinder your relationship with Christ. These things intrude into your relationship with the Lord and have no place there.

A sinful woman poured precious oil upon Jesus' feet and

then used her hair to wash His feet. (See Matthew 26:6–13.) It was an act of intimacy to give something of herself that was most prized, especially by a woman in her day. Her hair was one of her most precious commodities—it was her covering and her glory.

Mary of Bethany sat at Christ's feet and listened intently. She found herself enthralled in what Jesus had to say. This same love and devotion seem lacking in us, the body of Christ, even in those of us who call ourselves intercessors. We find ourselves busy praying, but not really listening to God. The many distractions in our lives typify Martha, who got upset with Mary and demanded that she share the busy tasks. She wanted to pull Mary into her own lifestyle and priorities. Martha felt she had a right to pull Mary away from her intimate walk with Jesus. This is what I see so often in the body of Christ. Many times we demand things of other people. We feel that people owe us and that we deserve more from them than what they give.

God values the kind of relationship that Mary and the sinful woman had with Him. The sinful woman was willing to break the alabaster box and rub oil on Jesus' feet. Others misunderstood her action and considered it to be a waste. My prayer is that people all across this nation will start to spend time alone with God so the spirit of the world will not distract them.

When we have nothing else to give, the demands of people control us because we feel obligated. This is not what God wants for us. Instead, He longs for us be like Mary and the sinful woman. Then we will be like broken bread and poured out wine for the hungry and thirsty. We will be like the oil inside the alabaster box that was poured out.

WILLING TO EXPERIENCE HOLY SEPARATION

WHEREVER WE PRAY, that place of prayer becomes a secret

chamber. It becomes our holy place. God expects us to have a holy, separated place where others are fearful to intrude.

We sometimes feel we can just come into the Lord's presence in any way we want and leave His presence in any way we want. But we must remember that the One we are approaching is holy. It is with a holy fear and an awesome reverence that we come into the presence of almighty God.

> Guard your steps as you go to the house of God, and draw near to listen rather than to offer the sacrifice of fools; for they do not know they are doing evil. Do not be hasty in word or impulsive in thought to bring up a matter in the presence of God. For God is in heaven and you are on the earth; therefore let your words be few.
>
> —ECCLESIASTES 5:1–2

We are to be prepared and made ready for the days ahead. Things that are unholy must not be permitted in our lives as we come before a holy God.

WILLING TO PRESS INTO THE SECRET PLACE

THERE IS MUCH to discover about the secret place of prayer in the presence of Jesus. This discovery requires perseverance to press into the Lord and to keep the things of this world out. The enemy will try to antagonize us and compete for the time we've set aside for God. Ask Him for victory to overcome the world, the flesh and the devil. (See 1 John 2:15–16.)

Sometimes our precious moments in the secret place of God's presence are intruded upon by telephone interruptions and other distractions. The enemy is an intruder. He likes to come when he is not invited. He is a trespasser with no right or privilege over us. And yet at times we allow his tactics to succeed, and we find ourselves pulled away from God's presence. We are not to be ignorant of his schemes (2 Cor. 2:11).

Take authority over this wicked intruder in the name of the Lord Jesus Christ that you may be set free and empowered to serve God. Many people in this world want to know Jesus Christ, but they are so busy in secular work or even the work of the ministry. How easy it is to be consumed by the world but not consumed by God's presence. Don't allow yourself to become consumed with the concerns of life to the exclusion of your relationship with Christ. No matter how good these things are, they are still not the best if God has little place or time in our lives.

WILLING TO CLEANSE OUR HEARTS FROM WICKEDNESS

WE WANT GOD to touch us, enrapture us and take us into the heavenlies, yet often we're not willing to remove the sin that He has revealed to us. We demand that He give us what we want when we haven't met the requirements to receive what we ask for.

> Therefore, since we have so great a cloud of witnesses surrounding us, let us also lay aside every encumbrance, and the sin which so easily entangles us, and let us run with endurance the race that is set before us.
>
> —HEBREWS 12:1

What hinders us when we come into God's presence, when we approach His throne carelessly? It is our sin. We must ask God to forgive us and take away the filthiness of our hearts, minds and self-will.

> If I regard wickedness in my heart, the Lord will not hear.
>
> —PSALM 66:18

WILLING TO EXEMPLIFY THE SPIRIT OF FORGIVENESS

THE CROWD THAT watched Jesus die on the cross didn't know what they were doing as they spat upon and mocked and cursed the Son of God. Jesus, in His passion, said, "Forgive them; for they do not know what they are doing" (Luke 23:34). When Stephen was being stoned, he did the same thing Jesus did by saying, "Lord, do not hold this sin against them!" (Acts 7:60).

Those who are intimate with Jesus will do the same when they are despised. They will say, "Forgive them, for they know not what they do." The crowd despised Stephen. They despised the love placed within his heart by the Holy Spirit. Those who desire to go the way of Jesus' passion must have a spirit of forgiveness no matter what the cost. Those who are despised for their passion for God will forgive deeply, even while being killed.

WILLING TO REJECT THE WORLD'S WINE

And when they had come to a place called Golgotha, which means Place of a Skull, they gave Him wine to drink mingled with gall; and after tasting it, He was unwilling to drink.

—MATTHEW 27:33–34

When we come into intimacy with Jesus, we no longer desire the world's wine, but only His. The world's wine no longer satisfies us. Jesus refused this drink because it was mingled with gall. It wasn't satisfying to Him; it could not quench His thirst, and neither could it take away His pain—it was bitter.

How many times have we gone to others to take away our pain? God wants us to turn to no one but Him to remedy our hurts and pain. Let us insist on a draught of that spiritual drink that represents the sweet communion of the Holy Spirit. No one can give us that but Jesus.

WILLING TO BE CHARGED BY OUR ENEMIES

And when they had crucified Him, they divided up His garments among themselves, casting lots; and sitting down, they began to keep watch over Him there. And they put up above His head the charge against Him which read, "THIS IS JESUS THE KING OF THE JEWS."

—MATTHEW 27:35–37

The lovers of God will be charged, they will be persecuted, they will be criticized and accused. (See Revelation 12:10.) At times accusations come from the enemy through the brethren in greater measure than from those of the world. Strong's definition of *charge* is "a cause (as if asked for), a reason or motive for a crime, an accusation, case, cause, crime or fault."

In Matthew 27:37, accusers made a charge against Jesus because of who He was. They judged His motives. They called Him names but didn't believe Him. Those who follow Christ's example will experience the same treatment. The crowd will accuse Christ's followers with cries of : "too spiritual…," "too heavenly minded to be of any earthly use…" and "too out of touch."

I thank You, Lord, that we can be spiritual and yet not out of touch with the world. You want us to be like eagles and fly (Isa. 40:31). You want us to be able to soar in the Spirit, to see the condition of the earth but to understand how to live above it. When others scold us and tell us to stop flying, help us, Father, to soar like an eagle—to soar like Christ.

The spirit of the world and the spirit of the enemy despises those who put the Lord Jesus first. We will be charged.

WILLING TO TAKE UP THE CROSS TO FOLLOW HIM

At that time two robbers were crucified with Him, one on the right and one on the left. And those passing by were hurling abuse at Him, wagging their heads, and saying, "You who are going to destroy the temple and rebuild it in three days, save Yourself! If You are the Son of God, come down from the cross." In the same way the chief priests also, along with the scribes and elders, were mocking Him, and saying, "He saved others; He cannot save Himself. He is the King of Israel; let Him now come down from the cross, and we will believe in Him."

—MATTHEW 27:38–42

God wants us to take up our cross daily and bear the reproach of unbelievers and the religious. We are to live that cross-bearing lifestyle and die daily to our own comforts, desires, pleasures, dreams and agendas. How will we know when we are bearing our cross? When we don't need to have people believe in us, exalt us and put us up on a pedestal. People wanted Jesus to come off His high place of the cross so He could be in a high place among the crowds. Those who walk the passionate walk can't walk like that. For those who walk the way of the cross, their elevation is the place of the cross. Our pinnacle will always be the cross—not ourselves. It is death to this life and death to much of what is acceptable to others. Our high place is a place of lowliness, brokenness and total submission to God.

Often we believers speak the world's language because we have the same mind as the world. Our minds have not been renewed by the Word of God. When we refuse to let go of self and our world, we do the same things to one another that they did to Jesus as He was dying.

Jesus could have used His power and wisdom to build a huge earthly following. Being passionately in love with the Lord and obedient to His commands involves risk. We may never gain great followings and the world's acclaim. Instead, we may be despised. When we go deeper in Christ, we risk becoming more unacceptable to the world and even to our brothers and sisters in Christ because of our separated lifestyle. When we are exclusively His, we bear His reproach in the world. We don't do what everyone else expects, but only what pleases Him. Our desire for popularity must die on the cross.

> He trusts in God; let Him deliver Him now, if He takes pleasure in Him; for He said, "I am the Son of God."
> —MATTHEW 27:43

The angry crowd mocked Him. They demanded that Jesus prove Himself to them. They looked for signs and wonders as proof of who He was and proof of His relationship with the Father. We don't have to prove ourselves to anyone but Him alone. And yet it's a temptation to do what looks right in the eyes of people.

> And the robbers also who had been crucified with Him were casting the same insult at Him.
> —MATTHEW 27:44

Being insulted and humiliated before others is part of the legacy of being a consecrated one. Satan, the accuser of the brethren, continuously finds fault. We will never measure up when we try. We will never meet the standard of others.

THE ONENESS JESUS SHARED WITH THE FATHER

Now from the sixth hour darkness fell upon all the land until the ninth hour. And about the ninth hour Jesus cried out with a loud voice, saying, "Eli, Eli, lama sabachthani?" that is, "My God, My God, why hast Thou forsaken Me?"

—MATTHEW 27:45–46

Jesus' heart broke when He was separated from Father God. No one has given themselves to God so totally as Jesus. No one on earth has had the kind of experience with the Father that Jesus has. For Him to be separated from the Father because of the sin He bore for us was unbearable.

THE BRIDE IS WILLING TO FOLLOW THE BRIDEGROOM TO THE END

And Jesus cried out again with a loud voice, and yielded up His spirit.

—MATTHEW 27:50

John 19:30 says, "It is finished!" Jesus made this proclamation at the point of death and completion of His divine purpose. There was nothing else to give—no more to be done. He had accomplished everything the Father required of Him. The world could now find salvation.

We too have to come to places of completion in our lives where we can say, "It is finished." Nothing has been left undone—our task is complete. Even in the spiritual work in which we may be involved, we will find a place of completion. At that point, we've given everything to the Lord and know in our hearts that it is finished. At other times we may sense that God has some unfinished business to be worked in us. God will often give us tasks that are too big for us to complete in the natural realm. Yet He expects us to give our all. When we have given of our own strength—all of our ability—and still come up lacking, God makes up the difference supernaturally. At the point of our weakness His strength is revealed.

I believe the Lord is bringing us, His bride, to a place where the work of our flesh is finished. This is how we are being prepared for glory in this life and the life to come.

WILLING TO LIVE THE RESURRECTED LIFESTYLE

And behold, the veil of the temple was torn in two from top to bottom, and the earth shook; and the rocks were split, and the tombs were opened; and many bodies of the saints who had fallen asleep were raised; and coming out of the tombs after His resurrection they entered the holy city and appeared to many.

—MATTHEW 27:51–53

The veil at the entrance to the holy of holies was rent open. After the death experience comes the resurrection lifestyle, when we are ready to be seen by the world. The world does not need to see us until then.

Intimacy with the Beloved is about the cross, dying and resurrection. "The tombs were opened; and many bodies of the saints who had fallen asleep were raised." Resurrection power comes in to birth fresh anointing, giftedness, power and all that we need to minister to the masses.

Now the centurion, and those who were with him keeping guard over Jesus, when they saw the earthquake and the things that were happening, became very frightened and said, "Truly this was the Son of God!"

—MATTHEW 27:54

When this resurrection life comes forth, we won't have to tell people who we are or what we have. Our lives will speak for the power, presence and resurrection life that is upon us.

The resurrection lifestyle will get the world's attention and win the world to Jesus. Others will seek us out. Even if we try to hide, just as Jesus did at times, people will search us out. The resurrection lifestyle is so genuine that people will start to respect Him in us. It is this lifestyle that will provide the platform we need to hold forth the Word of God. The body of Christ will have the world's attention and respect. The resurrection life of Christ will also bring the fear of God. Our very presence will bring a fear of God upon others. We will be so broken that the life of Christ will radiate from us with a burning fire.

WILLING TO RISK THE LOSS OF REPUTATION

And many women were there looking on from a distance, who had followed Jesus from Galilee, ministering to Him, among whom was Mary Magdalene, along with Mary the mother of James and Joseph, and the mother of the sons of Zebedee.

—MATTHEW 27:55–56

These wonderful women—Mary Magdalene, Mary the mother of James and Joseph and the mother of the sons of Zebedee—were willing to minister to Jesus during tribulation at great risk to their own reputation. They became outcasts. It was unsafe to minister to Jesus, and yet these women risked their lives and their reputations. Jesus, who had been God over all the earth, laid down His reputation and became a servant for the sake of His bride (Phil. 2:7).

Don't worry about a reputation. Rather, be willing to give it up, because it's part of the price. Those who seem to be the lowliest are the ones who will receive us. Are you willing to be despised for your passion? Are you willing to be misunderstood because you don't fit someone's traditional ideas? Are you willing to be cast aside, or to just not fit in? Being fitted where God wants us in the body of Christ may not be where we thought we should fit. But each of us has a different calling and a different function in the body. And the purpose of our lives is not to please people but to please God.

WILLING TO BE CHANGED AND TRANSPLANTED

SOMETIMES GOD UPROOTS us. He doesn't want us planted where we are anymore—He wants to plant us someplace different. Some will attempt to keep us where they think we fit best. We may even do this to ourselves. However, when we are close to the Lord and listening to His voice, we are continually being transformed. And when we are transplanted, it's usually for a higher purpose. We go from glory to glory, from one stage of growth to the next, and we need to be uprooted. We have to be replanted in a different pot, so to speak, to be expanded.

During the crucifixion of Christ, onlookers stood at a distance and watched. People are always watching to see where you will fall or how you respond to failure. The Lord may allow certain things to happen in your life because He wants a greater presence and glory to come forth in you. If you don't learn the lessons God puts in your path, you will not be your best, and you'll never attain all that He calls you to be.

WILLING TO SUFFER THE LOSS OF ALL THINGS

Now on the next day, which is the one after the preparation, the chief priests and the Pharisees gathered

> together with Pilate, and said, "Sir, we remember that
> when He was still alive that deceiver said, 'After three
> days I am to rise again.'"
>
> —MATTHEW 27:62–63

After Jesus died, some said He was the Son of God and others said He was a deceiver. When you live in the fellowship of Christ's suffering, some will say you're a deceiver. (See Philippians 3:10.) We cannot concern ourselves with changing other people's minds. Our job is to keep presenting Jesus and leave the rest up to His Holy Spirit. It is the Holy Spirit's responsibility to reveal who Jesus is.

Philippians 3:7–8 says, "But whatever things were gain to me, those things I have counted as loss for the sake of Christ. More than that, I count all things to be loss in view of the surpassing value of knowing Christ Jesus my Lord, for whom I have suffered the loss of all things, and count them but rubbish in order that I may gain Christ." In Strong's, the word *rubbish* means "what is thrown to the dogs, i.e. refuse, dung." Paul spoke of losing everything in order to gain Christ. Rejection and ridicule are in store for those who passionately love the Lord. Spiritual pride will make people ridicule us as well. Some people prefer the stench of pride to the fragrance of godliness experienced in humility.

Are you broken? Do you desire to be humble and willing to take the backseat? Only the Holy Spirit can place this desire within you.

WILLING TO UNDERGO THREE DAYS OF DEATH

> Therefore, give orders for the grave to be made secure
> until the third day…
>
> —MATTHEW 27:64

When we go through our death process, a symbolic three days are involved. I believe the Lord allows us time to die before we experience His resurrection power. During this time it seems there's no life, no joy—only death, darkness and pain. It feels as if there's no way out. You might call this the dark night of the soul in the daytime of life, or *the sixth hour.*

Matthew 27:45 says, "Now from the sixth hour darkness fell upon all the land until the ninth hour." The sixth hour was noon; the ninth hour was 3 P.M. "And about the ninth hour Jesus cried out with a loud voice, saying..." (v. 46). In the ninth hour, you are also ready to cry out. Sometimes we go through times when we don't feel, sense or see anything. It's as though we're dead. Then at the ninth hour, we cry out to the Father for help. After the times of darkness, crying out and death comes the resurrection life. God knows what it takes to make us die and what it takes to make us come alive again.

WILLING TO GO OUT AND MAKE DISCIPLES

MATTHEW 28:16–20 PROCLAIMS the Great Commission. The resurrection life of Christ within us makes us able to walk in the same authority that was given to Jesus. The resurrection life gives us a desire and ability to go out and make disciples to duplicate ourselves.

Jesus commands us to go out and disciple people, to mentor them in the Spirit. The passionate walk with Christ matures us and brings us to a place where we are able to multiply. We cannot give people something we don't have, and we cannot take them through a process if we haven't been there before them. An intimate walk with the Lord brings forth maturity and perfection in the spiritual realm. It is one of the key answers to evangelism. This crucified walk, where we are despised for our passion, is what makes us fit for evangelism.

SECTION 11

THE PATHWAY

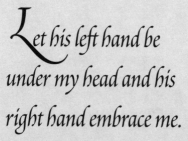

$\mathcal{L}$et his left hand be
under my head and his
right hand embrace me.

—SONG OF SOLOMON 2:6

4

The Unseen Hand

HAVE LIVED IN the guest cabin for almost two weeks now while writing this book. Each day has been an adventure. I awake each day with a fresh anticipation of what the Lord will speak to me. Two things awakened me this morning: the daylight breaking through the windows and the unmistakable hovering of the Lord's presence, which put a smile on my face and laughter in my soul. Joy comes in the morning! (See Psalm 30:5.)

The hovering of the Holy Spirit is like a brooding; it's the Lord overshadowing me with His blessed presence. (See Luke 1:35.) My Beloved is wooing me and covering me with His oil of joy. His presence is unmistakable to me.

I had sought Him through the night with all my heart in prayer and the Word. Now I had found Him. The Lord delights in confirming His Word and answering our prayers. As I found Him in those blessed moments, I held on, treasuring each second in His presence. If I had to stay in that room all day, so be it. I would not come out or stop until the Lord stopped. This time was too special to interrupt until He decided it.

> And I said, "Have you seen him whom my soul loves?"
> Scarcely had I left them when I found him whom my
> soul loves; I held on to him and would not let him go.
>   —SONG OF SOLOMON 3:3–4

His divine touch is like an unseen hand. He supports me with His left hand and embraces me in strength with the right. I cry out at times for joy because His holy presence fills my soul to overflowing.

When the Holy Spirit comes in this way, who can contain the joy of His marvelous presence? Sometimes the touch of His Spirit goes down into the depths of my soul, into the innermost chamber of my being. New life and vitality bubble up within me, transforming my soul.

Following such an encounter, others notice the transformation and ask, "What has happened to you?" I can only answer that I have been touched by the hand of God.

Each touch of His hand is for a different purpose. You are on a journey, discovering more about the nature of God. His unseen hand embraces, caresses and covers you as when Moses saw the glow of God's glory while he was hidden in the crevice of the rock. "And it will come about, while My glory is passing by, that I will put you in the cleft of the rock and cover you with My hand until I have passed by" (Exod. 33:22). The covering of His divine presence reminds you of His tender care and lovingkindness.

THE GREAT PHYSICIAN'S HAND

HOW CAN YOU explain a living encounter with the unseen

hand of God? It is unexplainable. His hand does something new in your mind and emotions. With the touch of His presence He takes you to a new level of healing and restoration. He gives you something that was not there before. He makes you whole, giving you a sense of well-being that you lacked before. If sadness lurked inside you, He overrides it with His deep joy and peace. You begin to laugh at the devil and all that he's trying to do. Your laughter becomes a weapon of warfare.

THE POTTER'S HAND

HIS TOUCH GENTLY molds you into a new piece of clay, strengthening you to walk unafraid of the night seasons of disappointment, discouragement, hurts, fears, frustration and loss. The Bible says, "'Can I not, O house of Israel, deal with you as this potter does?' declares the LORD. 'Behold, like the clay in the potter's hand, so are you in My hand, O house of Israel'" (Jer. 18:6).

The hands of our divine Potter mold and shape us. The Word of God says, "But now, O LORD, we are but clay, and Thou our potter; and all of us are the work of Thy hand" (Isa. 64:8). We are God's own precious work of art. We are His skillful handiwork. Each touch of His Spirit bears the imprint of a supernatural artist, molding us into the likeness of Jesus Christ.

Do you feel hidden from the world around you? Do you know with certainty that God has placed much within you that the people around you cannot see? He longs to put you on display before the world, to show the wonderful treasure of His craftsmanship hidden deep within you.

THE HAND OF BLESSING

AFTER YOU'VE WRESTLED with God like Jacob for the purpose

of obtaining His blessing, He strokes away your fear of the future and the unknown.

> Then Jacob was left alone, and a man wrestled with him until daybreak. And when he saw that he had not prevailed against him, he touched the socket of his thigh; so the socket of Jacob's thigh was dislocated while he wrestled with him.
>
> —GENESIS 32:24–25

You need not be afraid of the night hours, because He will light the way. "In Him there is no darkness at all" (1 John 1:5). God touched Jacob on his thigh, and for the rest of his life he walked with a limp. It was God's mark, but it was not a mark of wounding. It was a mark of blessing. As with Jacob, God leaves a mark of blessing upon our hearts. When you wrestle in the Spirit through the night in prayer, you receive a new name and identity. Your weakness becomes your strength as you acknowledge that your help comes from the Lord. This blessing, like Jacob's limp, is the mark that identifies you as God's own. You find that you are not taking yourself so seriously all the time. You are able to accept your imperfections more easily.

Your walk in Christ is unique. His brand upon your life tells others you have been bought with a price. Your life testifies to others that you are not your own. This blessing brings a new appreciation for the weakness in yourself and the strength that is only in God.

The mark of weakness is not given to identify you with the world. Instead, the mark of weakness from God's hand of blessing makes you beautiful in His sight. You are identified as His own possession. You now have God's beauty mark. You are God's property.

This was true when you first accepted Jesus as your Lord

and Savior. Now after experiencing the good and bad of this life for a while, you have a greater revelation of this fact. Jesus, our Beloved, was marked and bruised (Isa. 53:5). He was pierced that we may possess our salvation, and now He has inscribed us on the palms of His hands (Isa. 49:16).

THE HAND OF FAVOR

ONE OF THE results of an intimate encounter with the Lord is that others desire what you have: a thirst for God and a joy that wells up in your soul. Unbelievers and believers alike are provoked to jealousy, wanting more of God for themselves. As you desire more of God, He becomes more desirable in you to others. Your presence makes a difference in the lives of those who are hurting. Your presence is a healing balm for a desperate world that doesn't know Christ. You bring peace to every place you go.

People have many hidden things locked up in their souls that bind them and make them unhappy. Sometimes these things are hidden even from themselves. We must be loosed and freed so that we can lead others to Jesus. He will touch their souls with His power and love and make them whole. A brief touch of His hand can change a lifetime of hurt and pain into a new beginning of hope.

THE HAND OF A MASTER BUILDER

THE BIBLE SAYS, "But we all...beholding...the glory of the Lord, are being transformed into the same image from glory to glory" (2 Cor. 3:18). Each time we experience His presence we leave our prayer room changed. With each stroke of His hand we are being shaped into a new person. We are being made better for His purposes, which are not fully understood at the present moment, but will be understood in time.

The Lord has a plan for each of our lives. He is developing in us a taste for eternity. This appetite for eternity, this passion for glory, increases with each divine encounter, spoiling us for anything less. We become willing to endure the trials required by Him to develop His character within us. Are you willing to allow Him to accomplish His complete work in you for all eternity?

THE HAND OF PREPARATION

WE ARE BEING made ready for the coming of Jesus Christ. God is making us, His Bride, without spot or wrinkle. With the touch of His unseen hand, He wipes away the flaws and scars inflicted upon us by this world.

This is an individual work. Yet He is doing a corporate work as well. He touches the masses, blesses them and makes them new. But He always does His creative work one by one. He sees us as individuals. We are very special to God. Jesus died for one as well as for all. His presence descends upon one alone as His presence descends upon a group. He made us for Himself, created in His own image for the purpose of fellowship with Him (Gen. 1:26).

THE HAND OF HIS FELLOWSHIP

WE HAVE THE privilege of experiencing God's presence in the Person of the Holy Spirit. The Bible says the Holy Spirit will be in us and abide with us. His infilling presence never leaves us. But the presence of God is manifested to us in greater and lesser degrees. At times, the sweet fellowship of His presence may seem elusive. One moment He is here, and the next moment He is gone, as in Song of Solomon 5:6: "I opened to my beloved, but my beloved had turned away and had gone! My heart went out to him as he spoke. I searched for him, but I did not find him; I called him, but he did not answer me."

Our behavior and our words can cause Him to linger, or we can cause Him to leave without realizing what we've done. In a split second, the presence of God may start to lift. But if our complete focus is on Jesus, we learn what it is that makes Him stay and what causes His presence to leave.

THE HAND OF CORRECTION

GOD'S HAND IS often tender, but it can also be heavy. In some cases, His heavy hand represents correction, which involves God's grace and tough love, as is demonstrated in the following Scripture passage:

> They sent therefore and gathered all the lords of the Philistines and said, "Send away the ark of the God of Israel, and let it return to its own place, that it may not kill us and our people." For there was a deadly confusion throughout the city; the hand of God was very heavy there. And the men who did not die were smitten with tumors and the cry of the city went up to heaven.
>
> —1 SAMUEL 5:11–12

God wanted the ark back, and His hand was heavy upon the people so they would put it back where it belonged. Because of the Lord's love, His hand is heavy upon us at times to make us do what's right. God's chastisement is a demonstration of His love for us. The ark represents the presence of the Lord and His covenant relationship with His people. His hand was heavy upon the Philistines to make them respect Him and put His presence back where it belonged. God wants us to bring back the ark of the covenant, that is, the presence of God. He always wants His presence in the appropriate place. He wants us to respect and honor His presence or anything that is symbolic of His presence.

THE SURGEON'S HAND

WHEN HIS PRESENCE comes, the Lord starts to reveal things that have been hidden from us and need to be corrected. Obstinacy is rebellion within us. *Obstinate* means "to be unreasonably determined to have one's own way; not yielding to reason or plea; stubborn; dogged; mulish." When God reveals sin and we acknowledge and confess it, He cleanses us. His unseen hand becomes the surgeon's hand that removes the rebellion in us. We must yield, permitting God to do surgery upon our hearts. Otherwise the fire of affliction will become our schoolmaster, teaching us to be broken and yielded to God's control.

God's presence always humbles the pride within us. We have so many things within us that the Lord doesn't even allow us to know. God reveals in Scripture that He will not let us know it all. He says:

> They are created now and not long ago; and before today you have not heard them, lest you should not say, "Behold, I knew them." You have not heard, you have not known. Even from long ago your ear has not been open, because I knew that you would deal very treacherously; and you have been called a rebel from birth.
> —ISAIAH 48:7–8

Sometimes He refines us as silver and gold. Other times we are thrown into the furnace of affliction. But God promises that when we are refined through severe testings, we will be delivered from those testings.

Behold, I have refined you, but not as silver; I have tested
you in the furnace of affliction. For My own sake, for My
own sake, I will act; for how can My name be profaned?
And My glory I will not give to another. Listen to Me, O
Jacob, even Israel whom I called; I am He, I am the first,
I am also the last.

—ISAIAH 48:10–12

In these verses God speaks about His rightful place of lordship in our lives. He is Lord. We learn about the lordship of
Christ as we walk in intimate fellowship with God.

Surely My hand founded the earth, and My right hand
spread out the heavens; when I call to them, they stand
together.

—ISAIAH 48:13

THE DELIVERER'S HAND

TO KNOW GOD is to realize His power over the earth, over
wicked spirits and over the lives of men and women. At times
God reveals His glory, and we can do nothing but cry out
"Holy!" Our voices join the chorus of angels and archangels
who worship Him in His glorious splendor.

Sometimes God waits for special moments to speak to us
about the promise of deliverance. He promised Israel deliverance even in her state of rebellion. His presence brings
deliverance and sets us free. We need God's deliverance from
our rebellious ways. Scripture says, "The heart is more
deceitful than all else and is desperately sick; who can understand it?" (Jer. 17:9).

Encounters with the Lord bring deliverance. Reading the
Word of God washes us. The Lord reveals to us the secrets of
our own hearts and sets us free from deep wounds and fears.

THE CLEANSING HAND

GOD IS CONSTANTLY ridding us of anything that separates us from fellowship and relationship with Him.

> Behold, the Lord's hand is not so short that it cannot save; neither is His ear so dull that it cannot hear. But your iniquities have made a separation between you and your God, and your sins have hidden His face from you, so that He does not hear.
>
> —ISAIAH 59:1–2

Sometimes we feel separated from God, as if He's hiding from us. The truth is that something lies between us, and that something is sin. Are we willing to pay the price of repentance so that God's presence can be revealed in our lives again? He is always there waiting; He will never leave you nor forsake you (Heb. 13:5).

Nevertheless, He allows us to be separated from Him at times so we might become desperate enough and humble enough to ask for forgiveness and cleansing. When we repent of our sins, we find that He no longer seems hidden.

THE WRITING HAND

> And when He had finished speaking with him upon Mount Sinai, He gave Moses the two tablets of the testimony, tablets of stone, written by the finger of God.
>
> —EXODUS 31:18

Once while sitting in a plane, the Lord spoke to me and said that my heart is like an open book with blank pages on which He would write. The Holy Spirit writes on the tablet of our hearts with His finger. As we read the Scriptures and receive the revelation of the Lord, He writes on our hearts, minds, wills and emotions. His finger starts to do surgery while He writes with indelible ink a message that cannot be washed away. When the finger of God writes upon our heart, we receive our life's message—the substance of our ministry.

You can't live your spiritual life through other people. You have to have your own personal walk with God and hear from Him for yourself. You must allow His finger to write on the tablet of your heart. You can learn from other people who help lead you to God, but when all is said and done, you must experience God for yourself. When you have been made ready and present yourself, the Lord will descend.

THE COVERING HAND

> Then the LORD said, "Behold, there is a place by Me, and you shall stand there on the rock; and it will come about, while My glory is passing by, that I will put you in the cleft of the rock and cover you with My hand until I have passed by. Then I will take My hand away and you shall see My back, but My face shall not be seen."
> —EXODUS 33:21–23

The covering hand of God is His presence and glory. God covered Moses with His glory as He passed by and revealed Himself. In our nakedness, God comes and clothes us with His glory—that is, His goodness. By nakedness I mean those hidden places in our hearts about which only He knows: our fears, our insecurities, our hidden pain. God covers us so that we are exposed to no one but Him.

> And the LORD descended in the cloud and stood there with him as he called upon the name of the LORD. Then the LORD passed by in front of him and proclaimed,

"The LORD, the LORD God, compassionate and gracious, slow to anger, and abounding in lovingkindness and truth; who keeps lovingkindness for thousands, who forgives iniquity, transgression and sin; yet He will by no means leave the guilty unpunished, visiting the iniquity of fathers on the children and on the grandchildren to the third and fourth generations." And Moses made haste to bow low toward the earth and worship. And he said, "If now I have found favor in Thy sight, O Lord, I pray, let the Lord go along in our midst, even though the people are so obstinate, and do Thou pardon our iniquity and our sin, and take us as Thine own possession."

—EXODUS 34:5–9

The intercessor stands as a priest before the most high God just as Moses did. In God's presence you stand in the gap and intercede on behalf of God's people. This is not only for your own fulfillment but for a higher purpose as well. Like Moses, certain things are required of us. Moses had to be ready at a certain time and place. He had to be ready to present himself alone.

God proclaimed Himself to Moses during this special encounter. Moses didn't proclaim who God was—God proclaimed who He was. "Then the LORD passed by in front of him and proclaimed, 'The LORD, the LORD God, compassionate and gracious, slow to anger, and abounding in lovingkindness and truth; who keeps lovingkindness for thousands, who forgives iniquity, transgression and sin…'" (Exod. 34:6–7).

THE MERCIFUL HAND

GOD REVEALED THE depth of His character and the wonder of

His nature to Moses with just a glimpse of His glory. Moses saw God in all His splendor and majesty.

How awesome it is to experience the grace of God, the fear of God, the justice and wrath of God, the mercy of God, the love of God, the truth of God, the kindness of God and the peace of God and not be annihilated. The goodness of God kept Moses alive in His holy presence. This is true holy ecstasy.

God's mercy triumphs over His judgment. When the Lord reveals unholy things in our lives, His mercy covers and protects us from His judgment because of the blood of Christ.

"And Moses made haste to bow low toward the earth and worship" (Exod. 34:8). That was his response to God. Then he stood in the position of priest and intercessor for his people. "And he said, 'If now I have found favor in Thy sight, O Lord, I pray, let the Lord go along in our midst, even though the people are so obstinate; and do Thou pardon our iniquity and our sin, and take us as Thine own possession'" (v. 9). Moses identified with the sins of his own people and repented on their behalf. This is standing in the gap in its purest sense. Moses presented these stiff-necked people to God. The role he played is a role that we intercessors perform today as well.

When God comes in His awesome glory, we will respond as Moses did. We will get down low and worship. God is passionately in love with us, and that's why He loves to hover over us, to weigh us down with His glory.

THE RIGHT AND LEFT HAND

He has brought me to his banquet hall, and his banner over me is love. Sustain me with raisin cakes, refresh me with apples, because I am lovesick. Let his left hand be under my head and his right hand embrace me.

—Song of Solomon 2:4–6

71

God's hands, His left and His right, are equally powerful and reliable. We can trust His hands. The *right hand* is the hand of strength, skill and authority. (See Job 40:14; Psalm 45:4; 137:5; Proverbs 27:16; Matthew 27:29; Revelation 1:16.) It is also a hand of love and tenderness. (See Song of Solomon 2:6; 8:3.) It bestows the greatest blessings. (See Genesis 48:13–18; Revelation 1:17.) The place of greatest favor, honor or influence is on the right. (See 1 Kings 2:19; Psalm 45:9; 109:6; Matthew 25:33.) It is the more important hand or side because it is the one by which a man is led. (See Psalm 73:23.)[1]

The *right hand of God* is a favorite Old Testament expression for God's almighty power in creation (Isa. 48:13); in war and deliverance (Exod. 15:6; Ps. 17:7; 18:35; 20:6; 44:3; 78:54; 98:1; 118:16; 139:10); and for His sovereign beneficence (Ps. 16:11; 48:10; 80:15, 17). To be seated at the right hand of God signifies a position of greatest honor, reserved only for the royal figure of Messiah. (See Psalm 110:1.)

The *left hand* is usually associated with warfare. The ability to use both hands equally was highly prized among the ancients, especially among warriors. (See Judges 20:16.)[2]

Sometimes a personal relationship with the Lord is like having a hand to hold in a crowd. We sense a blessed security that He is there for us, and we are not alone. We don't have to do anything spectacular, but only walk with Him and let Him lead the way. When we hold hands, our hearts meet as well. A divine trust comes with the touch of His unseen hand.

*F*or one who speaks in
a tongue does not speak to
men, but to God.

—1 CORINTHIANS 14:2

5

The Language of Love

ONE OF THE most precious gifts the Holy Spirit gives is the gift of tongues. It's the language of love and war. It's a personal language of intimacy with the Lord as well as a weapon of spiritual warfare. Yet this gift is neglected and misunderstood. It has been called the language of ecstasy throughout the ages, and those who have exercised it have often been considered imbalanced, unintelligent or even possessed by other spirits. Paul said, "I thank God, I speak in tongues more than you all..." (1 Cor. 14:18). He was not ashamed of this gift in his life, but he wanted to make sure he used it appropriately before God and men. Personally, I don't know what I would do without this blessed gift from heaven.

THE LANGUAGE OF FIRE

THE BOOK OF Acts uses the term "tongues of fire." This gift is exactly that—it is both fire and power! The gift of tongues is also a language of passion. When speaking this language of love you may sense a fire burning in your spirit that empowers and empassions you to worship, praise, pray and do God's will.

THE LANGUAGE OF OFFENSE

THE GIFT OF tongues offends and is thought by many today to be no longer relevant. The reason it offends is because it offends the enemy. Satan knows the power of the tongue to do good or evil (James 3:5–10). This language is often used to give praises to God, which the enemy hates and cannot understand. It offends the mind and intellect of those who are afraid to release their innermost hearts to God for fear of appearing foolish. You have to be willing to be a fool for Jesus to exercise the gift of tongues. It requires a humble heart and a yielding to Him.

THE LANGUAGE OF POWER AND AUTHORITY

I WOULD NOT deny this gift for anything in the world. Tongues is a gift that has been given to me straight from Jesus by His Holy Spirit. In some circles this wonderful prayer language is almost forgotten; many feel little need for it and believe it has lost its significance. We need tongues now more than ever. We need tongues to do warfare as well as to express our love, worship and praises to God.

The gift of tongues can be a primary tool of communication to the Lord in our prayer closets. It relates through the spirit to the heart of God from the heart of God. It's powerful because it speaks the mysteries and secrets of the Holy Spirit. With this language, we can express ourselves to God beyond our own limited intellects (1 Cor. 14:2). When our minds can no longer articulate, our spirits take over—further and deeper—a perfect language of prayer and worship.

THE LANGUAGE OF THE HOLY SPIRIT

THROUGH THE GIFT of tongues, we're able to express the heart and mind of the Holy Spirit to and from the Father. I believe that those who desire greater intimacy with the Lord know instinctively that this gift will help them greatly. Many who are deeply intimate with God lack this prayer language, but I encourage anyone who is open, even to a small degree, to seek God for this gift.

It's probably one of the most neglected gifts today among Charismatics and Pentecostals. Some who have the gift of tongues have lost the fire that should accompany it. Such individuals experience a dryness within as they speak in tongues out of obedience. Are you in need of fresh fire? Keep being obedient—dedicate more time to praying in tongues and worshiping Jesus in the Spirit as often as possible. Your fire will come back.

Though we may pray in the Spirit in English as well, we need to experience the day of Pentecost all over again. Every day should be a day of Pentecost. At the house of Cornelius in Caesarea, believers spoke with tongues (Acts 10:46). John's disciples at Ephesus spoke in tongues when they believed (Acts 19:6). Some Bible commentators believe the gift of tongues occurred also in Samaria (Acts 8:17–18).

THE LANGUAGE OF HEAVEN

THE GIFT OF tongues is a language of heavenly worship and love to God. It should operate by love. And when this language is spoken in love, it accomplishes great victory in warfare.

The gift of tongues is a language of heaven, of men and of

angels; it should be spoken with love (1 Cor. 13:1). No wonder the enemy tries to keep us from using it. Satan hates the use of tongues because it penetrates the spiritual realm. While using this gift we are speaking about the holy things of God. We're using the language that helps bring down the glory of God. This language helps us to draw near to God because we speak to God and not to men, except when there is interpretation (1 Cor. 14:2).

The gift of tongues is a language of command—God's command—because we are speaking by the power of the Holy Spirit. Terror strikes the enemy's heart. Yet even so, it's also a language of humility. One has to let go of pride and be as a child in order to express this gift. It's a language of power and authority expressed through humble lips.

THE LANGUAGE OF RENEWAL AND REST

THE GIFT OF tongues is the language of refreshing, revival, renewal and rest. (See Isaiah 28:11–12.) It's even the language of reconciliation between you and God because of the intimate communion with Jesus. When a person speaks in an unknown language, he or she is communicating with perfect praise and worship to the Lord. This can only happen as you are in one accord with the Holy Spirit. This language of the Spirit woos the heart of the Father. It also woos ours.

The gift of tongues has been a noisy gong and a clanging cymbal at times, but it can also sound an alarm and call forth the army of God. When we pray in tongues to God, He responds and sends help.

We need not be ashamed of the gift of the Holy Spirit. This precious gift should be used mostly in the secret place—in the prayer closet between you and God. However, at times our prayer language should be used in the corporate setting, with interpretation for the whole body of believers, or without interpretation while all lift their voices to God in worship and warfare. Oh, what glory is experienced when an entire congregation lifts up their voices in the language of love and war! Thousands of demons flee. The spiritual atmosphere is cleared.

THE LANGUAGE OF INTIMACY

THE GIFT OF tongues is a language of intimacy that expresses delight to do God's will. It's a language of submission, obedience and humility. (See 1 Corinthians 14:15.) Some feel foolish when they speak in tongues. But when you are in love, you don't mind feeling a little foolish. On the day of Pentecost the believers who spoke in tongues were thought to be drunk. Using this language can cause you to become intoxicated by the presence of God.

Romans 8:26–27 speaks of "groanings too deep for words." I believe these groanings at times may be the gift of tongues operating by the unction of the Holy Spirit. These groanings are also literal groans, moans, lamentations and utterances that are too deep for words—just varied sounds that only God Himself understands.

THE LANGUAGE OF ANOINTING

NOT ONLY DOES an anointing fall on the speaker of tongues, but also on the hearer of tongues to interpret what was spoken. Many years ago I prayed for my sister to receive the baptism in the Holy Spirit. When I started to pray in tongues, the anointing came upon her, and she interpreted everything I said. (See 1 Corinthians 12:10, 30; 14:13, 27.) She had never heard about interpretation. She didn't know much about the gifts of the Holy Spirit. She was a new believer, brand-new in spiritual things.

In her spiritual ears she heard an English interpretation as I spoke in an unknown tongue. The Holy Spirit anointed my mouth to speak in another language and anointed my sister to hear and interpret, just as on the day of Pentecost. She looked at me and listened with surprise as she heard the interpretation in English. God gave her the understanding. Shocked, she said to me, "I heard and understood what you said!" My sister experienced an anointing to interpret the language of the Holy Spirit.

THE LANGUAGE OF ETHNIC SPEECH

GLOSSALALIA, OR SPEAKING in tongues, not only means "foreign languages spoken miraculously" by those who have never learned them, but also "ecstatic language and ethnic speech."

Receiving this heavenly language is a matter of asking God for it. Often I've heard stories of missionaries who went to a group of people without knowing their native language, and the Holy Spirit empowered them to speak in the native tongue. This miracle from God still happens in our present day.

Sometimes a person who doesn't have the time to learn a language can actually learn it in a supernatural way. God gives such supernatural abilities to an individual by the power of the Holy Spirit as He thinks best.

THE LANGUAGE OF EVIDENCE

SPEAKING IN TONGUES is one of the evidences of the baptism of the Holy Spirit, but I don't believe it's the only one. The gift of tongues is an outward sign of an inner work of the Holy Spirit. The inner work must occur before the outward sign manifests.

Three thousand responded and believed on the day of

Pentecost, and tongues were the sign to those who were saved that day. Could tongues be a sign for unbelievers today? I believe so.

Tongues validate the messenger as well as the message. You can see why the enemy tries to stop us from praying in tongues. The following two scriptures bear this out:

> Men of Israel, listen to these words: Jesus the Nazarene, a man attested to you by God with miracles and wonders and signs which God performed through Him in your midst, just as you yourselves know…
> —ACTS 2:22

> The signs of a true apostle were performed among you with all perseverance, by signs and wonders and miracles.
> —2 CORINTHIANS 12:12

Tongues were a sign to the unsaved in Acts 2:11 and a sign to the believing Jews that Gentile believers were received by God in Acts 10. In Acts 19:2–6 the gift of tongues validated the reality of the Holy Spirit in their lives.

> In the Law it is written, "By men of strange tongues and by the lips of strangers I will speak to this people, and even so they will not listen to me," says the Lord. So then tongues are for a sign, not to those who believe but to unbelievers; but prophecy is for a sign, not to unbelievers but to those who believe.
> —1 CORINTHIANS 14:21–22

THE LANGUAGE OF EDIFICATION

THE LORD GIVES the gift of tongues as a language of faith and edification, or building up. The one who speaks in a tongue edifies himself (1 Cor. 14:4). Praying in tongues is a beautiful way to express ourselves to Christ and also to build ourselves up in the Holy Spirit. The definition for *edify* is "to be a house builder, i.e. construct or (fig.) confirm: (be in) build (ing, up), edify, embolden." I find the phrase, "to be a house builder," quite exciting. We have the Creator of all the universe living inside our spiritual "house."

THE LANGUAGE OF DEVOTION

LET US BUILD our house in prayer and deep devotion to Christ by praying in this language of devotion. The gift of tongues is the perfect language of praise: ". . . and let him speak to himself and to God" (1 Cor. 14:28).

We have the ability to commune with the Lord privately in our hearts in tongues, even while we're with others. In 1 Corinthians 14:18–19, Paul said, "I thank God, I speak in tongues more than you all; however, in the church I desire to speak five words with my mind, that I may instruct others also, rather than ten thousand words in a tongue." Paul knew the value of tongues better than most. This gift was so precious that he was careful not to misuse it in public. Nevertheless, he did not neglect it in private. He knew it was important that others reverence it as well. If someone feels led to speak in tongues in a corporate setting, and there is no interpreter, he can remove himself when the groans prevail. Sometimes the Holy Spirit moves upon the corporate body as one, and all are moved with groanings in the Spirit.

Paul cautioned us not to prohibit tongues, yet he also saw the dangers of misusing tongues. I believe the use of tongues by the body of Christ has been hindered because we've focused more on its problems than its benefits. When something is powerfully used by the Holy Spirit, we tend to focus on the negative things that come with it instead of the positives, and so the enemy hinders or stops us completely. We would rather have everything perfect, with no mistakes, than to have the Holy Spirit operating in us and have to do a little clean-up later. We all make mistakes and will learn along the way, by God's grace.

THE LANGUAGE OF PROPHECY

WHEN USED IN public, the gift of tongues is coupled with the gift of interpretation. The gift of tongues is not used very frequently in public settings with interpretation because it's seldom used in private or small-group settings. This is just a lack of practice. First Corinthians 14:40 says, "But let all things be done properly and in an orderly manner." My prayer is that we will not quench the Holy Spirit in ourselves or in others, because the relationship we have with the Holy Spirit is a progressive revelation of Jesus Christ. There is so much more to know.

Paul listed four things in Scripture concerning tongues and its practice:

1. It is intended to edify or build up those present.
2. No more than two or three should speak at a time.
3. Tongues should be spoken in turn, not simultaneously.
4. If no interpreter is present, the speaker of tongues should keep silent. (See 1 Corinthians 14.)

When a person has spoken a message in tongues in a public setting, usually he waits for someone with a prophetic gift to interpret. I believe that if God gives an individual the anointing to speak in tongues in a public setting, He will also give them the interpretation by the Holy Spirit if no one else interprets.

THE LANGUAGE OF AN EXPECTANT BRIDE

THE GIFT OF tongues was given to us as the bride of Christ while we eagerly await our Bridegroom. We need not lack in His giftings. In 1 Corinthians 1:7, Paul said, "…so that you are not lacking in any gift, awaiting eagerly the revelation of our Lord Jesus Christ."

We need everything we can get until His coming. In some ways we've been robbed in the body of Christ during the past several years. God desires unity in the body. We must be careful when we come together with others so we don't offend. We should be willing to lay down some of the gifts we use in our own spiritual circles when we come together with others who disagree with our beliefs. Unity in the Holy Spirit is that important. However, we must also be careful not to go to the other extreme and deny God's gifts in us.

The gift of tongues is never to be our focus. Jesus is the greatest gift of all. When our tongues are genuinely from Him, they will glorify Him, always point to Him and reveal His mind and heart. Remember, though, that tongues will stir some to offense. Scripture says, "…and greater is one who prophesies than one who speaks in tongues" (1 Cor. 14:5). Therefore, some have erroneously felt it has no value. However, the gift of tongues is a powerful, secret weapon of the Holy Spirit. When we speak in tongues, the enemy doesn't know what we're saying. He cannot interpret it.

THE LANGUAGE OF PRAYER

I PRAY THAT God will stir up the gift of tongues inside you and rekindle the fire of the Holy Spirit. I pray that God's mind, will and emotions will be manifested in you as you pray and praise in tongues—the perfect prayer language of the Holy Spirit. If you desire to receive this gift, I pray that you would not be hindered by your intellect or pride, but instead be in total submission to Jesus Christ. Ask and receive that your joy may be full. Open your mouth wide, and let the Holy Spirit fill it. Lay down your inhibitions, and speak out by faith. No one is looking. You are in the presence of an audience of One—Jesus.

We are not limited because we don't always understand what we're saying. God hears us and understands our prayer language. When we speak in tongues, we enter into a spiritual realm where we touch the miraculous. What a thrill it is to experience visions, dreams, signs and wonders!

Praying in tongues can be a continuous dialogue between you and God. I like to wake up in the morning praying in tongues. I like to fall asleep praying in tongues. Often I sense that my spirit is praying in tongues deep inside of me.

Acts 2:4 says that the Spirit gives us *utterance,* which means to "enunciate plainly, to declare or to speak forth." The Holy Spirit gives us the ability to speak, and we partner with God to express outwardly a spiritual language of the inner man. We're using our own vocal cords, our own sounds, our own tongue and our own lips. But God Himself gives us the ability to formulate the words.

THE LANGUAGE OF HEAVENLY EMOTION

EVERY HUMAN EMOTION imaginable is expressed through the gift of tongues under the direction and power of the Holy Spirit. These are emotions that God Himself expresses at times. When the Spirit of the Lord moves upon us, we may enter into His emotions and feel what He feels. We enter into a wonderful accord with the heart of the Father.

> Give ear to my words, O LORD, consider my groaning.
> Heed the sound of my cry for help, my King and my
> God, for to Thee do I pray. In the morning, O LORD,

> Thou wilt hear my voice; in the morning I will order my
> prayer to Thee and eagerly watch.
>
> —PSALM 5:1–3

Every human emotion found in the Book of Psalms can be expressed in our own lives under the unction of the Holy Spirit. Even negative emotions, those we're afraid to express, are also discovered in the Book of Psalms, which is a book of prayer and praise. God understands every emotion expressed inwardly and outwardly. He understands every groan, grunt, sigh, whimper, wail, whoop or utterance from the human heart. He understands every unintelligible sound, expression or emotion of the spirit. He created sound. First Corinthians 14:10 says, "There are, perhaps, a great many kinds of languages in the world, and no kind is without meaning."

The language of love and war is a language of unhindered communication with God. God Himself laughs, shouts, sighs, whispers, whistles, sings, weeps, cries out, moans, groans and more. God laughs at His enemies and whistles for the nations. "He who sits in the heavens laughs, the Lord scoffs at them" (Ps. 2:4). "He will also lift up a standard to the distant nation, and will whistle for it from the ends of the earth; and behold, it will come with speed swiftly" (Isa. 5:26).

I encourage you to press in a little deeper and discover anew, or perhaps for the first time, this wonderful gift of tongues with all its exciting benefits. Expand in your spiritual expressions through the language of heaven, love and war.

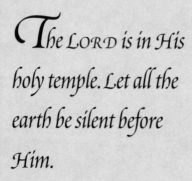

The LORD is in His holy temple. Let all the earth be silent before Him.

—HABAKKUK 2:20

6

Silence: A Key to the Throne Room

ONE NIGHT WHILE a group of us were at dinner, there was silence for a couple of minutes. Some seemed to feel uncomfortable and tried to keep the conversation going by asking questions and telling stories or jokes. We're often uncomfortable in silence with others, in silence with ourselves and in silence with God. Heaven, however, has a very different response to silence. As you journey into deeper levels of intimacy with God, you will discover that silence is a powerful instrument of heaven. Often it is silence that activates, releases and precedes the greatest spiritual benefits into your life.

I used to think prayer was talking to God. That is one definition of prayer, but I discovered years ago that prayer is more than talking. It's a relationship that has more to do with communication than with mere words or phrases. Yes, words are for the purpose of communication, but what is coming from the heart—or spirit—is more important. Sometimes our words don't express our hearts adequately. With God's help, our words will start to line up with our hearts.

For many years I would pray in the early hours of the morning and meet with my Lord. One day I discovered that I didn't have to do all the talking. As I waited and listened, I found myself in silence in God's presence for hours. Some days I sat in silence for one to four hours, and other days for eight hours or more. I wasn't watching the clock, but when the anointing lifted I would be amazed at how much time had passed. On special, personal retreats that I take throughout the year, I would experience several days of silence and yet still be in blessed communication with my beloved Lord Jesus. Many times I felt I had seen and tasted heaven. Perhaps I did, who knows? Only God knows.

John the Beloved had a revelation of Jesus Christ and said in Revelation 1:10, "I was in the spirit on the Lord's day...." Paul described a vision in 2 Corinthians 12:2–4, saying, "I know a man in Christ who fourteen years ago—whether in the body I do not know, or out of the body I do not know, God knows—such a man was caught up to the third heaven. And I know how such a man—whether in the body or apart from the body I do not know, God knows—was caught up into Paradise, and heard inexpressible words, which a man is not permitted to speak." What can I say here? The Lord still moves upon men and women in this way today and will do so in the future. We have become too cynical and full of unbelief. If the Lord wanted to bring us into this experience, would we allow Him to do so? Perhaps this is your day for a heavenly visitation. Who knows? God knows.

SILENCE: A KEY TO HEAVEN

And when He broke the seventh seal, there was silence in heaven for about half an hour. And I saw the seven angels who stand before God; and seven trumpets were given to them. And another angel came and stood at the altar, holding a golden censer; and much incense was given to him, that he might add it to the prayers of all the saints upon the golden altar which was before the throne. And the smoke of the incense, with the prayers of the saints, went up before God out of the angel's hand. And the angel took the censer; and he filled it with the fire of the altar and threw it to the earth; and there followed peals of thunder and sounds and flashes of lightning and an earthquake.

—REVELATION 8:1–5

In Revelation 8:1–5, we witness a scene in the throne room of God in heaven. We see angels as an integral part of the kingdom business here on earth through prayer and worship. The seventh and eighth chapters of Revelation reveal a pattern of worship that leads to silence. You will discover that the Spirit will often lead you in this way. It begins with high praises to God accompanied by great swells of worship with shouts of excitement, and it ends in an awesome, holy hush.

This silence is pregnant with a sense of expectancy as you receive a fresh revelation of God's sovereignty. This worship experience is not only for the corporate body of believers, but it can be experienced during one's own personal time alone with God.

SILENCE: A KEY TO RELEASING THE VOICE OF GOD

DO YOU DESIRE a prayer life of greater intimacy with the Father? I encourage you to take time to be still before God and let Him speak to you. As you wait before God, His voice will become increasingly clear to you. He speaks into our spirit-man. But even when He is speaking, He doesn't always articulate in words. At times we will have an impression; at other times a picture or vision will flash into our hearts. The Lord may impart something to us, and later He will explain what He has done. God also speaks to us through His Word as we sit and read, letting it digest within our quieted souls.

In this passage of Scripture, there was silence in heaven, and the saints offered up prayers upon the golden altar before the throne. The saints had God's complete attention. Smoke from the incense that accompanied the prayers of the saints ascended before God by the angels' hands. I believe that angels assist in the presentation of our prayers to God in ways that we will not understand until we see our Lord face to face.

SILENCE: A KEY TO ACTIVATING THE PRAYERS OF THE SAINTS

IT SEEMS TO me that during this wonderful scene of heavenly intercession God already knew what He wanted to do. He was just waiting for the prayers to be activated. When the silence came, great activity followed. As heaven fell into a hushed silence, the prayers and petitions of the saints on earth were placed before God's throne.

As all heaven waited in holy stillness, the answers to those prayers and petitions erupted, breaking the silence with the power of God's response.

SILENCE: A KEY TO RELEASING DELIVERANCE

MOSES SPOKE TO the people of Israel as they were fleeing from Pharaoh and the Egyptians: "The LORD will fight for you while you keep silent" (Exod. 14:14). Deliverance is accomplished for us as well when we are still before the Lord. Silence is an act of faith in prayer; it is a peaceful rest revealing a heart that trusts in God, fully assured that He will do what He has promised.

A certain series of events occurred before the angels were activated. It appears that when enough prayers had come up to the throne of God, the Lord released angels to accomplish the requests. The Lord spoke the word, sending angels from heaven in response to the prayers of the saints on earth.

> Then the Lord awoke as if from sleep, like a warrior overcome by wine. And He drove His adversaries backward; He put on them an everlasting reproach.
>
> —PSALM 78:65–66

When we are led of the Holy Spirit to be silent, God is a mighty warrior stirred to bring deliverance on our behalf.

Many do not consider that those who are quiet and contemplative in prayer are engaged in spiritual warfare. We have assumed that the more loudly we pray the more powerful the effect. It is never the noise that causes victory in prayer. Deliverance comes as we obey the Holy Spirit's promptings, regardless of whether they are loud or soft. It's not a matter of how loudly or softly we pray. What matters is the strategy that God is using at that given moment in time.

Silence is a weapon of warfare. Silence is a strategy in warfare. Silence *is* warfare. God Himself operates in the midst of our silence, fighting the battle for us.

SILENCE: A KEY TO RELEASING DIRECTION IN PRAYER

WE CAN'T MAKE God do anything, but we can ask in prayer. We can pray and believe until we experience the hand of God moving on our behalf. Silence allows us to hear and to sense how to move forward in prayer.

Silence is a rested spiritual state into which we enter after we've poured out our hearts to God, knowing deep inside that He has heard us. Worship, followed by intercession that flows into a restful silence, is a pattern of heavenly prayer. When we pray in the Holy Spirit we are lifted into that heavenly pattern, and it is duplicated here on earth by the Spirit of God.

How glorious it is to be completely caught up in the Holy Spirit just as the saints and angels were in the Bible. At this very moment saints in heaven are worshiping and praising God. We on earth are one church together with them, bound by the power of the Holy Spirit. We on earth, together with those saints in glory and the angels around the throne, can enter into their spiritual worship, glorifying God as one great cloud of witnesses.

That heavenly cloud of witnesses is having a ball up there dancing before Him, shouting and praising His name. Don't wait until you attend a big meeting with crowds of people. Worship and exalt Him when you are alone in your prayer closet with the same fervor as you would in a crowd of thousands.

SILENCE: THE KEY TO RECEIVING DIRECTION IN BIBLE STUDY

JUST GET ALONE with your Bible and read it in God's presence. The power of the Word of God will help motivate you into a deeper walk with the Holy Spirit. I've taught for years that it is vital to use the Word of God in prayer. When you get alone with the Lord, always have your Bible open. Bible reading and prayer are inseparable. Read during prayer; read prayers from out of the Bible. Take the prayers of the great saints and make them your own.

Bring a prayer journal into your prayer closet along with your Bible, and record the thoughts, feelings, prayers, petitions and prophetic insights you receive there. Doing this can change your life. It can cause you to understand your own thoughts and fears as your mind becomes renewed by the Word of God.

Do you long to receive a fresh word from God to share with your congregation or Sunday school class? Almost all of my teaching material has come through this method of prayer. I've learned to pray until I sense a clear direction from the Lord on what to teach or speak. When I've tried to preach without prayer, I find myself struggling or unable to teach. I go before the Lord and wait in silence until I receive what He wants me to speak about.

As God directs you in your study of the Word, He'll give you a little leading—perhaps a word or idea will rise up in your spirit. I've learned never to ignore such promptings. If it's a single word, I'll look it up. If it's a scripture, I'll open my Bible and read it. Then I'll pray and wait until I sense something more. Soon the revelation of insight from the Word of God will begin to flow into my waiting heart. In this way I've learned to draw from the depths of the Holy Spirit's wisdom.

As you wait, pray, read and write—receiving fresh insight from God—you will find that your inner man will grow increasingly sensitive to the Holy Spirit's whispers, and you will begin to live in a continual flow of revelation from God.

When you have learned through silence to allow God to become your counselor, you will discover that the Holy Spirit will also use you to counsel others. At the moment a weary soul needs encouragement, a fresh "word in season" will rise up in your heart—all because you've learned to silence yourself before God, and you've learned to listen and draw from His wisdom. Too often we blurt out things before we've quieted ourselves and given thought to our words. Silence is vital because it prepares you to hear the still, small voice of God, even His whisper.

SILENCE: A KEY TO COMMUNICATION WITH GOD

GOD GETS OUR attention in silence, and when we are silent we get His. Some people believe they must keep talking in order to communicate. However, the absence of noise is not necessarily the absence of communication. With God you don't have to do or say anything. He communicates quite well without words.

When you are silent before God, you are saying, "It's Your turn now." This is just good manners and shows reverence. This is the communication of two persons who love each other deeply, not two acquaintances who talk noisily.

God's silence is not just an absence of words, but a deep communion with Him through His Spirit. Some synonyms for silence are *stillness, calm, peace, hush, secrecy.* Another synonym for silence is *decrease.* In John 3:30, John the Baptist said, "He must increase, but I must decrease." Silence brings us to a place of quiet, decreasing us so that Jesus can increase in us. We are full of ourselves at times, always feeling we have something to say. By continually talking we make ourselves the center of attention. By growing silent before God, we make Him the center of our attention. We decrease through our silence.

SILENCE: A KEY TO SUBMISSION

SILENCE IS NOT speaking so that He can speak. Silence helps bring us to a place of submission to His Word, ways, thinking and lordship.

With silence comes an understanding of God that can't be expressed in words—it is simply a knowing and a being. In silence you discover what it means to be still and know Him with a divinely revealed knowledge. In silence we experience what the psalmist declared in Psalm 46:10: "Cease striving and know that I am God; I will be exalted among the nations, I will be exalted in the earth." The King James Version says, "Be still, and know that I am God."

SILENCE: A KEY TO HEALING

A DEEP WELL of God's presence resides in the inner being of every Christian. And in that well of God's Spirit flows a fountain of healing. As we quiet our flesh, that fountain of living water will spring up within us, overflowing our souls with the virtue of God. It is through stillness and silence that we tap into those healing springs of God's Spirit.

In stillness before Him, the Healer, *Jehovah Rapha*, takes control. He rises up within us, making us whole as we wait before Him in silence.

It's interesting to note that a synonym for silence is *to propitiate*. This means to cause to become favorably inclined, and to make atonement or propitiation. One of the key words for propitiation is satisfaction. "And He Himself is the propitiation for our sins; and not for ours only, but also for those of the whole world" (1 John 2:2). As we wait upon our Lord in silence, we realize that He has satisfied or silenced our debt of sin with His shed blood.

SILENCE: A KEY TO UNSPEAKABLE JOY

SILENT PRAYER BEFORE the Lord is not an outward thing. This communion is expressed in a deep connection of your heart to God's heart, your spirit to God's Spirit. This relationship is communicated from Spirit to spirit. Silent prayer is active listening—it is communication without words. It is deep prayer that fills the heart with unspeakable joy—a joy that brings divine rest to your soul.

SILENCE: A KEY TO BRINGING OUR TONGUES
AND THOUGHTS UNDER CONTROL

I DO A lot of teaching on different types of fasting, and people are always amazed when I encourage them to fast from talking. We fast and deny our bodies food, bringing our bodies under subjection to the will and purposes of God. Why not fast from talking?

The Lord says we're going to give an account one day for every word that comes out of our mouths. There is a safety in silence as we guard our tongue. Most of us tend to finish someone else's sentences for them. I'm a much better listener now than I used to be. But I still need work in this area. Our tendency is not to really listen to someone thoroughly. We are thinking ahead before they finish and not listening to their heart. When we're with God, we need to listen to His heart.

Being silent helps put our tongue in subjection to the Holy Spirit. Bringing our tongue under control is a form of self-discipline. Why do we feel we always have to speak? Why do we always think about the next thing we will say during our conversations? Let's allow God to speak to us instead; let's allow Him to fill our minds with His thoughts.

When you become truly quiet, a song of worship will often rise up in your spirit. The more we look at Jesus, the quieter we become and the more we stop thinking about what we can do and say next. After a while, we discover that Jesus consumes our whole mind. At that point all we can think about is the Lord. Silence is golden, and it is precious. Psalm 62:1–2 says, "My soul waits in silence for God only; from Him is my salvation. He only is my rock and my salvation, my stronghold; I shall not be greatly shaken." In silence and stillness we will be fortified so we will not be shaken—our thoughts will not roam wildly into fear, and our tongues will not lash out in ungodly ways. Silence is a powerful key in bringing our thoughts and words under the control of the Holy Spirit.

> For though we walk in the flesh, we do not war according to the flesh, for the weapons of our warfare are not of the flesh, but divinely powerful for the destruction of fortresses. We are destroying speculations and every lofty thing raised up against the knowledge of God, and we are taking every thought captive to the obedience of Christ, and we are ready to punish all disobedience, whenever your obedience is complete.
>
> —2 CORINTHIANS 10:3–6

Silence helps us to bring every thought captive to the obedience of Christ. It puts the enemy to flight, and it silences him. But when we silence our tongue, eventually our mind—with its vain imagination and arguments that exalt themselves above the will and purposes of God—is brought under control. Not only does Scripture say that a soft answer turns away wrath, but it also says to agree with our adversaries quickly. Sometimes we don't have to defend ourselves or do anything. We don't have to say anything at all.

SILENCE: A KEY TO CONTEMPLATION AND MEDITATION

> On God my salvation and my glory rest; the rock of my strength, my refuge is in God. Trust in Him at all times, O people; pour out your heart before Him; God is a refuge for us. Selah.
>
> —PSALM 62:7–8

I heard the Holy Spirit speak to my heart these words:

"Silence is the *selah* of God." Silence before God is a form of contemplative prayer. So many people are afraid of the words *contemplation* and *meditation*. Practicing silence before the Lord in prayer will take you high into the heavenlies and deep into the heart of God.

While you pray in silence, listen to the silence. Silence is a gift. There is power in silence. There is also a reverential fear of God in silence. Silence is a time to regroup, rethink, reevaluate and reflect. Silence is the *selah* of God. *Selah* is a musical or liturgical interlude. *Selah* is God's musical interlude, pausing in the symphony of life to stop, look, listen, and take some time to think about what has been sung. In silence there is music, and God has a song.

SILENCE: A KEY TO GAINING NEW STRENGTH

Beware of the barrenness of a busy life.

—ANONYMOUS QUOTE

Our lives are so hurried and busy. When too much activity swirls around us, sometimes it is best just to stop and get quiet. God actually commands us to keep silent so we can gain new strength (Isa. 41:1). Then we may speak and receive His counsel and judgment.

Have you ever been around a person who says very little, yet when he or she does speak everyone seems to pay attention? Such people have a quiet demeanor; they have no need to be always talking. They exude a quiet, peaceful confidence and strength.

Isaiah 65:24 says, "It will also come to pass that before they call, I will answer; and while they are still speaking, I will hear." This passage of scripture implies that we do not have to speak about our needs, concerns and fears. In our silence God hears us—even without our opening our mouths. And before we speak it out, He is already answering. The Lord already knows what we need. We don't have to strive in our hearts, seeking to be heard by God. We are already heard. We need only to rest in this wonderful assurance.

SILENCE: THE 'KEY TO 'VICTORY

SILENCE IS A weapon of warfare. When the Spirit of God draws you into a place of silence, the Lord is saying, "It is time for you to stop fighting and let Me fight. You just be quiet. You go sit down. I'll take care of the matter."

That warfare is in spiritual battle, and the victory is won in silence. When we are silent in prayer, we still the strength of our flesh. When we do, the Lord becomes the warrior inside of us. The strength of God, a power much greater than what our flesh could ever produce, is manifested within us.

> Now Jericho was tightly shut because of the sons of Israel; no one went out and no one came in. And the LORD said to Joshua, "See, I have given Jericho into your hand, with its king and the valiant warriors. And you shall march around the city, all the men of war circling the city once. You shall do so for six days. Also seven priests shall carry seven trumpets of rams' horns before the ark; then on the seventh day you shall march around the city seven times, and the priests shall blow the trumpets.
>
> "And it shall be that when they make a long blast with the ram's horn, and when you hear the sound of the trumpet, all the people shall shout with a great shout; and the wall of the city will fall down flat, and the people will go up every man straight ahead."
> . . . But Joshua commanded the people, saying, "You shall not shout nor let your voice be heard, nor let a

word proceed out of your mouth, until the day I tell you, 'Shout!' Then you shall shout!"

—JOSHUA 6:1–5, 10

These verses are powerful. They teach us that there is a time to be silent, and there is a time to shout (Eccles. 3:6). We miss God because we're often shouting when we should be silent, or silent when we should be shouting. Sometimes we have to be silent, and at other times we need to shout. We must be extremely sensitive to the Holy Spirit. Joshua commanded the people to make sure they did not let a word proceed out of their mouths until the appropriate time in order to win the battle. They obeyed him and won.

SILENCE: A KEY TO GENTLE BLOWING

Then he came there to a cave, and lodged there; and behold, the word of the LORD came to him, and He said to him, "What are you doing here, Elijah?" And he said, "I have been very zealous for the LORD, the God of hosts; for the sons of Israel have forsaken thy covenant, torn down Thine altars and killed Thy prophets with the sword. And I alone am left; and they seek my life, to take it away."

So He said, "Go forth, and stand on the mountain before the LORD." And behold, the LORD was passing by! And a great and strong wind was rending the mountains and breaking in pieces the rocks before the LORD; but the LORD was not in the wind.

And after the wind an earthquake, but the LORD was not in the earthquake. After the earthquake a fire, but the LORD was not in the fire; and after the fire a sound of a gentle blowing. And it came about when Elijah heard it, that he wrapped his face in his mantle, and went out and stood in the entrance of the cave.

And behold, a voice came to him and said, "What are you doing here, Elijah?" Then he said, "I have been very zealous for the LORD, the God of hosts; for the sons of Israel have forsaken Thy covenant, torn down Thine altars and killed Thy prophets with the sword. And I alone am left; and they seek my life, to take it away."

—1 KINGS 19:9–14

Although no one can see the Lord and live, God passed by Elijah as he waited silently in a cave. Before God appeared to Elijah, a number of powerful things preceded Him—a great wind, an earthquake and a fire. Interestingly, the Bible says that the Lord was not in these things. The Lord was in the "gentle blowing," a very special place requiring silence before God. That "place" is seldom frequented by God's people.

We won't hear the gentle blowing until we get quiet. God speaks to us in a still, small voice. In the hum of noise all around us, we must draw silent before God to hear this gentle blowing of His Spirit. We will never enter the place of His presence while we are talking, when our minds are filled with self-centered thoughts and our hearts are encumbered with hectic activity.

SILENCE: A KEY TO RECEIVING DIRECTION, CORRECTION AND INSTRUCTION

WHEN WE BECOME quiet before God, we are able to receive the revelation of His presence that Elijah received. We can also receive direction, correction and new instruction as Elijah did. Remember that Jezebel was chasing Elijah. Spiritual warfare and demonic activity surrounded him. Have you ever felt as if the devil were chasing you relentlessly? Have you ever felt that spiritual warfare was breaking out all around you? In these moments it's more important than ever to draw silent before God in order to receive clear direction.

When we're quiet we can hear God's still, small voice. The very next thing that happened to Elijah was that he received direction.

> And the LORD said to him, "Go, return on your way to the wilderness of Damascus, and when you have arrived, you shall anoint Hazael king over Aram; and Jehu the son of Nimshi you shall anoint king over Israel; and Elisha the son of Shaphat of Abel-meholah you shall anoint as prophet in your place. And it shall come about, the one who escapes from the sword of Hazael, Jehu shall put to death, and the one who escapes from the sword of Jehu, Elisha shall put to death."
>
> —1 KINGS 19:15–17

After this time of silence, Elijah heard the still, small voice of God and received instruction about his next assignment. That's what God will do for us as well; He will give us our instructions for our next assignment.

> "Yet I will leave 7,000 in Israel, all the knees that have not bowed to Baal and every mouth that has not kissed him." So he departed from there and found Elisha the son of Shaphat, while he was plowing with twelve pairs of oxen before him, and he with the twelfth. And Elijah passed over to him and threw his mantle on him. And he left the oxen and ran after Elijah and said, "Please let me kiss my father and my mother, then I will follow you." And he said to him, "Go back again, for what have I done to you?" So he returned from following him, and took the pair of oxen and sacrificed them and boiled their flesh with the implements of the oxen, and

gave it to the people and they ate. Then he arose and
followed Elijah and ministered to him.

—1 KINGS 19:18–21

In the midst of spiritual warfare, the devil had succeeded
in isolating Elijah, causing him to feel alone and abandoned.
Despair settled over his soul, and out of the darkness of that
battle against witchcraft Elijah cried out, "I alone am left."
The devil had nearly defeated him. But when he drew near to
the Lord through silence, God opened his eyes and broke
the darkness of the lies that had been cast over his mind.

God reminded Elijah that he wasn't alone; seven thousand others had not bowed before the demonic oppression
that sought to enslave the people of God.

If you'll take time to silence yourself before God even in
the midst of your greatest struggles, He will not only give you
direction but remind you that He's taking care of it all. One
of the characteristics of an intimate walk with God is more
rest and peace and a greater realization that God does the
battling on your behalf.

Out of that gentle blowing came direction, encouragement, strength and rest. Elijah also received correction. God
gently reminded him that he was not the only "big cheese"
there. And that's what silence will do. It will put you in your
place and make you see how small you are, how big God is
and that God has everything under control.

SILENCE: A KEY TO
RECEIVING A CALL TO MINISTRY

WHEN GOD APPEARED, Elijah received instruction for his next
assignment. The Lord might even show you your replace-
ment. To whom are you going to pass your mantle?

Following this encounter with God, Elijah threw his mantle

over Elisha. He was willing to give away what he had. When you spend time waiting upon God and listening to His voice, you become empowered to give away what He's given you.

The mantle represented Elijah's anointing. Such encounters with God empower you to go out and impart to others what God has given to you. After a time of silence and waiting upon God, you are equipped to go and impart. That's what Elijah did, and that's what ministry is all about.

SILENCE: A KEY TO THE ANOINTING

ELIJAH SOUGHT THE Lord when he felt all alone. He became convinced in his heart that he was the only one left in Israel who hadn't sold out to Baal. When he told God how alone he felt, the Lord kept him alone for a longer stretch of time until a mighty breakthrough come into his life.

We're never really alone when God is with us. This is a powerful truth that Elijah learned all over again. It's only in the depths of God that you learn you're not alone. God knows your every need. He showed Elijah in prayer that seven thousand others had not bowed the knee to Baal. Following this wonderful encouragement, God provided Elisha to travel with him and minister to him. In the depths of God's presence, God met Elijah's needs spiritually, emotionally and physically.

SILENCE: A KEY TO GOD'S ARISING

"Sing for joy and be glad, O daughter of Zion; for behold I am coming and I will dwell in your midst," declares the LORD. "And many nations will join themselves to the LORD in that day and will become My people. Then I will dwell in your midst, and you will know that the LORD of hosts has sent Me to you. And the LORD will possess Judah as His portion in the holy land, and will again choose Jerusalem. Be silent, all flesh, before the LORD; for He is aroused from His holy habitation."

—ZECHARIAH 2:10–13

These powerful verses speak about God's favor coming to His people. It cautions all flesh to be silent before the Lord, for He is aroused from His holy habitation. When we shut up, God stands up. When we are silent before the Lord, He is stirred from His holy habitation to come and to do His mighty works on our behalf.

When an intercessor lies down to pray, God stands up to move in his or her behalf. When we stop talking and stop doing, we have come to a place of pure expectancy in God (Ps. 62:5). Then God is aroused from His habitation; He begins to move in power on our behalf.

What is it that makes us feel we must always be doing something? That we have to do everything? We don't. We don't have to do anything at times. Sometimes God's strategy is for us to do and say nothing, fully trusting in His ability to move every mountain.

SILENCE: A KEY TO STANDING AGAINST ACCUSATION

And those who had seized Jesus led Him away to Caiaphas, the high priest, where the scribes and the elders were gathered together. But Peter also was following Him at a distance as far as the courtyard of the high priest, and entered in, and sat down with the officers to see the outcome. Now the chief priests and the whole Council kept trying to obtain false testimony against Jesus, in order that they might put Him to death; and they did not find any, even though many false witnesses came forward. But later on two came forward, and said, "This man stated, 'I am able to destroy the temple of God, and to rebuild it in three days.'"

And the high priest stood up and said to Him, "Do You make no answer? What is it that these men are testifying against You?" But Jesus kept silent. And the high priest said to Him, "I adjure You by the living God, that You tell us whether You are the Christ, the Son of God."

Jesus said to him, "You have said it yourself; nevertheless I tell you, hereafter you will see the Son of Man sitting at the right hand of Power, and coming on the clouds of heaven." Then the high priest tore his robes, saying, "He has blasphemed! What further need do we have of witnesses? Behold, you have now heard the blasphemy; what do you think?" They answered and said, "He is deserving of death!"

—MATTHEW 26:57–66

When Jesus stood against His accusers, He was silent. When He spoke, He did not make excuses or defend Himself. Have you ever wondered why He didn't speak up? He had such great wisdom. Why didn't He answer their accusations? Father God was His defense.

Jesus' strategy before Pilate, the chief priests and elders was to remain silent. There are times when we need to do the same thing. When others are pointing the finger and accusing you, respond with silence. Great power is found in that. When you refuse to defend yourself, God will rise up to defend you.

At times, no defense you could make will help you against the power of Satan's accusations. The natural man will always believe a lie or the negative first. But God will move heaven and earth to come to your defense against the devil's accusations. Silence at such times is difficult, but Jesus proved it to be a powerful weapon against the enemy of our souls.

SILENCE: A KEY TO WISDOM AND UNDERSTANDING

Then the LORD said to Job, "Will the faultfinder contend with the Almighty? Let him who reproves God answer it." Then Job answered the LORD and said, "Behold, I am insignificant."

—JOB 40:1–4

This is what happens when we're quiet and God speaks: We become insignificant in our own sight. This reveals a perfecting of our understanding. Next to God we are nothing—He alone is everything. When all is said and done, there is nothing we can say.

Job arrived at a place in which he realized he had nothing to say. He had spoken; his friends had had their say. And finally God spoke. When He speaks, we become silent. Our silence says, "All right, God; You're the boss. Next to You I am nothing."

Then the LORD answered Job out of the storm, and said, "Now gird up your loins like a man; I will ask you, and you instruct Me. Will you really annul My judgment? Will you condemn Me that you may be justified? Or do you have an arm like God, and can you thunder with a voice like His? Adorn yourself with eminence and dignity; and clothe yourself with honor and majesty. Pour out the overflowing of your anger; and look on everyone who is proud, and make him low. Look on everyone who is proud, and humble him; and tread down the wicked where they stand. Hide them in the dust together; bind them in the hidden place. Then I will also confess to you, that your own right hand can save you."

—JOB 40:5–14

In silence we recognize who God is and what we are not. It's at this point of realization that true wisdom is born in our hearts. Silence gives birth to wisdom and understanding.

> Then Job answered the LORD, and said, "I know that Thou canst do all things, and that no purpose of Thine can be thwarted. 'Who is this that hides counsel without knowledge?' Therefore I have declared that which I did not understand, things too wonderful for me, which I did not know. 'Hear, now, and I will speak; I will ask Thee, and do Thou instruct me.' I have heard of Thee by the hearing of the ear; but now my eye sees Thee; therefore I retract, and I repent in dust and ashes."
>
> —JOB 42:1–6

In silence, Job's heart became wise. In silence, Job truly saw God. Over and over again in the Bible we see that when we come before the Lord and silence our flesh, we arrive at an open door of revelation. It is in silence that we truly let go, truly stop seeing self and, often for the very first time, truly see God.

SECTION 111

THE
PURPOSE

The news about Him was spreading even farther, and great multitudes were gathering to hear Him and to be healed of their sicknesses. But He Himself would often slip away to the wilderness and pray.

—LUKE 5:15–16

7

Rendezvous
With the Beloved

I T WAS THE custom of Jesus to go out preaching and
teaching, diligently doing the work that God had
entrusted to Him. But in the midst of the many pressures
that pulled at Him, He would often slip away to spend time
alone with God. I believe this was the secret of His love relationship with the Father. This is the secret that can keep our
relationship as well.

SLIPPING AWAY TO PRAY

IT'S IMPORTANT TO get away with the Lord, to have times
committed to seeking Him for hours and days without inter-
ruption. I call such times *a rendezvous with Jesus.*

A *rendezvous* is "a meeting between two or more persons set by an appointment." By the Lord's grace, my desire
in this chapter is to motivate you to present yourself to the
Lord, slipping away often for rendezvous—special times set

aside for communion with your heavenly Bridegroom.

RENDEZVOUS IN A LITTLE COTTAGE ON THE SOUND

I HAVE JUST arrived from spending three days at Barnam Point. During my stay there, I rested, slept, walked and enjoyed God's creation. Most of my time was spent in prayer—prostrate on the floor—fasting, listening, reading, waiting on God and even wrestling with Him. As I sat on the porch and waited in the quiet, I could hear the sound of fish leaping up out of the water and birds diving down to skim the surface for their dinner. One evening a huge owl flew down and perched on the edge of the roof for a rest. I looked up and was delighted to see it. I saw other wildlife as well.

Whatever God had in mind for me there seemed to be completed, and now I knew it was time to move on to the little cottage on the sound, situated on the west side of Camano Island, Washington. I felt that God was leading me to change my place of rendezvous. He was leading me to know where to go, when to stay and how long to stay. Surrounded by spectacular sunsets every evening and majestic trees that created a feeling of sanctuary, I rendezvoused with Jesus. I felt that my wrestling was over. I took a sigh of relief and relaxed.

A PLACE OF REFLECTION

THE BIBLE MENTIONS presenting ourselves before the Lord—coming apart or coming away to meet with Him. *Webster's* says *rendezvous* means "to present yourself." When you rendezvous with your heavenly Bridegroom, you present yourself before Him full of expectancy that He will meet you there as well.

The word *rendezvous* is derived from the French word

rendre, which means "to deliver." When you have a rendezvous, you deliver yourself over to someone else. When you have a rendezvous with your heavenly Bridegroom, you give yourself totally to Him.

A PLACE OF PREPARATION
TO BECOME FISHERS OF MEN

A RENDEZVOUS CAN be a place where the vessels of a whaling fleet meet at the end of a season to transfer their catch to a schooner. We are called to be fishers of men. (See Matthew 4:19; Mark 1:17.) How interesting it is that the disciples encountered Jesus at the seaside as well. Their encounter with Jesus prepared them to become fishers of men, as our encounters with Jesus prepare us for the same purpose. Just like the whaling vessel's rendezvous, we are entrusted to transfer our catch of souls to others for their growth and development.

A PLACE OF HIDING BEHIND
THE CLOUD OF GOD'S PRESENCE

A RENDEZVOUS WITH Jesus is also a time set apart for retreat and refuge. During times of warfare it's common for navel ships to rendezvous to mobilize forces and decoy ships away with an additional fleet.

When we take refuge, it serves a purpose, creating a decoy to catch the enemy off guard. A powerful tool of spiritual warfare is to go into the hiding place of God's presence, retreating in order to receive instruction from God. It also disarms the enemy. Satan tries to make us think we are not on the job when we take a retreat. Nevertheless, going into retreat is a major part of our job description and should not be neglected.

We can be deceived when we're always busy doing, going and running. How often we're busy with much activity but are not very effective in the purposes of God. It feels as if we're doing a lot. But sometimes the enemy watches and sees that we're burning ourselves out.

A rendezvous is God's smoke screen—His cloud behind which we're hiding. By coming apart in God we grow more effective in battle. God is looking for quality, not always quantity, in what we produce in our lives. It is the enemy of our souls who drives us, heaping increasing loads upon us, constantly demanding more while sapping our strength with the weight of many concerns.

The burden God gives us is light (Matt. 11:28–30). When we come into God's presence, we are giving Him our load. We cease bearing our burden alone, and we discover the blessed strength of God's shoulders lifting the weight of our burden.

A PLACE OF MOBILIZING GOD'S FORCES

THE MILITARY USES times of retreat to mobilize its forces. Having a rendezvous with the Lord and gathering with one or two other brothers and sisters to seek the Lord in prayer can also accomplish this.

A rendezvous with the Lord as a group should precede the launching of every new ministry venture, every building plan and every major change in direction of your ministry or career.

How often have we discovered from hindsight that we went down the wrong path or did not receive all of the Lord's strategy for launching a new ministry venture? Setting time apart for the purpose of prayer and pressing into God can also knit hearts together. This can ensure unity later on when attacks come and Satan tries to divide and destroy what God is attempting to do through you. Sometimes the enemy thinks we're hiding from him, when instead we're really mobilizing with others who have joined us.

A PLACE OF REFRESHMENT

RENDEZVOUS IS A time to listen, to get fresh orders and to be refueled. We come into the hidden place with Jesus to receive His mind and heart. Instead of sweating to do the work entrusted to us, we begin to operate as priests. In a rendezvous, the Holy Spirit prepares us for what lies ahead with keener discernment.

A PLACE OF REST

WHEN WAS THE last time you had a rendezvous with God? In business we realize it's essential to have "R and R." One of the devil's strategies is to wear out the saints. (See Ephesians 6:11.) He knows when we're about to run out of steam. It would really shock him if we broke our pattern of constantly *doing* and took the challenge of getting off by ourselves for a rendezvous with the Lord.

So often we are afraid to leave our ministries and church responsibilities. Many pastors are afraid to leave their churches for a week or more. They're afraid they might return and find a church split or a takeover. They might find that someone has usurped their authority or that important tithers have left the church.

Ministers who are too fearful to take time off to meet with the Lord miss the opportunity of becoming even more empowered—something the enemy hates most of all. No wonder the devil strives to keep us anxious and busy working. We fear that if we dare to stop, productive activity will cease. We're afraid that things might get so far behind that we'll never be able to catch up.

Things are going to get behind anyway, but God is still on the throne, and He will help us do the things that are necessary. He will supernaturally empower us to be efficient with our time. He will also bring others whom we can trust to support us and empower them for the task.

A PLACE TO BE REFUELED

A RENDEZVOUS IS also a place where ships are refueled. Rendezvous is a place for us to be refueled. Where did Jesus go to be refueled? In rendezvous with the Father.

> And in the early morning, while it was still dark, He arose and went out and departed to a lonely place, and was praying there. And Simon and his companions hunted for Him; and they found Him, and said to Him, "Everyone is looking for You." And He said to them, "Let us go somewhere else to the towns nearby, in order that I may preach there also; for that is what I came out for." And He went into their synagogues throughout all Galilee, preaching and casting out the demons.
>
> —MARK 1:35–39

During Jesus' ministry, He traveled, healed, delivered, preached and yet still took time in the early morning hours to rendezvous with the Father. He knew to come to the Father *before* ministry and *after* a ministry event.

> And the apostles gathered together with Jesus; and they reported to Him all that they had done and taught. And He said to them, "Come away by yourselves to a lonely place and rest a while." (For there were many people coming and going, and they did not even have time to eat.) And they went away in the boat to a lonely place by themselves.
>
> —MARK 6:30–32

They were so busy they didn't have time to eat. In Mark 1 Jesus went alone by Himself, but then His disciples came looking for Him. In Mark 6, He came away to a lonely place—this time with His disciples. He took His inner circle, a select few, with Him. But they were so busy they didn't have time to eat.

A PLACE OF EMPOWERMENT

But He Himself would often slip away to the wilderness and pray.

—LUKE 5:16

Are we receiving from Him enough of what we need to be more effective when we go out? One of the keys to rendezvous with the Father is to get in a lonely place. Jesus spent time away with His disciples. But probably more often than not He slipped away to the wilderness alone and prayed. Jesus spent His days pouring out His strength and releasing the power of God upon the crowds. He touched sick bodies with the anointing of God's presence, sent demons to flight with the strength of holy unction and battled attacks from His enemies with wisdom straight from heaven. As a man, how did He find the strength? By always taking the time to get alone with His Father.

A PLACE OF WISDOM

And it was at this time that He went off to the mountain to pray, and He spent the whole night in prayer to God. And when day came, He called His disciples to Him; and chose twelve of them, whom He also named as apostles.

—LUKE 6:12

Although Jesus' days were busy ministering to people, it appears He also felt a great need to get with the Father and draw upon His wisdom.

When persecutors assaulted Him with their rage, how was it that He always had an answer filled with wisdom, grace and peace? He responded to the world's folly with heaven's grace.

But what happens to us? Sometimes people come against us or speak against us. Sometimes people surround our lives, draining us, pulling from us everything we have. God is saying to come away for a few hours. Go out to the mountain and pray; spend the entire night alone in prayer to God.

A PLACE OF PROVEN LOVE

DO YOU LOVE Jesus enough to spend quality time with Him? Often we think our love for Jesus is proved by being out there with the masses. But if we love Him so much, we should want to spend time with Him.

Do you love Jesus so much that you are compelled to pull away from the crowd, even when they're in need? There comes a time when evangelizing, healing, teaching and training people is no longer blessing God. Sometimes it's no longer even blessing you or the people to whom you're "ministering." Is this the ministry with which God is pleased?

We must have the other aspect of our ministry—ministry unto Him. A rendezvous with Jesus says we love Him more. Are we willing to hear what *He* has to say instead of what *others* have to say? Are we willing to spend time with Him over and above anyone or anything else?

Is He our first love (Rev. 2:4)? Do we desire to make Him a priority? Have we forsaken all for Him?

A PLACE OF WATCHFULNESS

I'M SITTING RIGHT across the bay from a marine base. I keep hearing the airplanes go overhead, followed by a beautiful silence. After I hear the silence I hear the airplanes again. I believe God is trying to say something here. Be watchful always. In the silence and in the noise, the watchman must be alert. Be prepared; don't be caught off guard.

> The end of all things is at hand; therefore, be of sound judgment and sober spirit for the purpose of prayer.
>
> —1 PETER 4:7

I believe God is calling forth a new kind of prayer warrior who has a greater sensitivity to the Holy Spirit. These new warriors are empowered with the weapon of God's love and the Word. They have a greater gift of discerning spirits, and they exercise prudence, wisdom and tact.

A U.S. Marine Corps general on a news program said that our military has a new generation of weaponry with a greater ability to hit targets with precision. The rendezvous is one of the best strategies to help bring about God's new generation of warriors who exercise greater precision with the weaponry of the Holy Spirit. (See 2 Corinthians 10:3–4; Ephesians 6:10–20.)

A PLACE OF PREPARATION FOR GLORY

THE VIEW TONIGHT of Puget Sound and the Saratoga Passage is spectacular. It's about 8:10 P.M., and I'm sitting and watching the sunset. My heart is filled with thankfulness to God for creating such beauty. One day we will have the greatest rendezvous when we meet the Lord in the air. When was the last time you thought about the glorious return of the Lord? The rendezvous we have now while on this earth is only a preparation for the greater rendezvous we'll have one day in heaven.

Now the sun has set, and the sky is blood red, which causes me to reflect on many different scriptures. The Bible speaks about the glorious return of the Lord.

> But immediately after the tribulation of those days the sun will be darkened, and the moon will not give its light, and the stars will fall from the sky, and the powers of the heavens will be shaken, and then the sign of the Son of Man will appear in the sky, and then all the tribes of the earth will mourn, and they will see the Son of Man coming on the clouds of the sky with power and great glory. And He will send forth His angels with a great trumpet and they will gather together His elect from the winds, from one end of the sky to another.
>
> —MATTHEW 24:29–31

I believe the Lord allowed me to see the sky tonight and its blood-red sunset to draw my attention to the Second Coming of Jesus. We need to be ready and looking for His coming. When are we to expect Him? A rendezvous puts more desire in our hearts to see Him, with a greater sense of anticipation. It helps to make us ready for His coming. It stirs the faith in us to believe He's coming back soon.

Nevertheless, no man knows the day or the hour. The blood-red sky I saw tonight makes His coming seem imminent. A bride is making herself ready, becoming spotless, and will rendezvous with the Lord in the air.

> And the Spirit and the bride say, "Come." And let the one who hears say, "Come."
>
> —REVELATION 22:17

A PLACE OF SANCTIFICATION

I SEE ANOTHER reason why it's so critical to have a rendezvous now before that great rendezvous in heaven. First Thessalonians 5:23 says, "Now may the God of peace Himself sanctify you entirely; and may your spirit and soul and body be preserved complete, without blame at the coming of our Lord Jesus Christ."

We are the bride of Christ, getting ready for the Bridegroom's soon return. How do we get ready? We become sanctified. *Sanctified* means "to set apart." By setting time apart to be with Him, we become set apart for Him. We become separated from the busyness of our daily activities and separated to Him alone.

Since I've been here on Camano Island, I've had a couple of encounters with people who believe they had another life. First John 2:28 says, "And now, little children, abide in Him, so that when He appears, we may have confidence and not shrink away from Him in shame at His coming."

This is the only life we have here, and the next one will take us into eternity forever. Hebrews 9:27 says, "And inasmuch as it is appointed for men to die once and after this comes judgment."

There is a great host awaiting us in heaven, cheering us on and waiting for us to come and join them (Heb. 12:1–2). One who has an intimate walk with the Lord desires to go and be with Jesus and looks forward to the day when he will join that great host.

PLANNING FOR A RENDEZVOUS

A RENDEZVOUS REQUIRES planning, with a prearranged time and place. You may decide to go away. Or this personal retreat could simply be a time alone in your house when you close the door, pull the blinds down, turn the phone and TV off and pretend you're not there.

You can choose a time frame for a certain period, such as an hour, a day, even a weekend. Decide what it is you want to get out of this time away with the Lord. It should have a meaningful purpose.

CHOOSE A PLACE THAT'S RIGHT FOR YOU

YOU ARE UNIQUE. What blesses you may not bless another. Your rendezvous will be unique because you are. Maybe you prefer to be on the beach. Maybe you like to go up into the mountains to spend time with God.

I often think about how Adam and Eve walked with the Lord in the garden, in the cool of the evening. Just imagine the wonderful shade that came from those trees after a heavy day's work. I love to go walking down paths in the woods, listening to the whistling wind blow through the trees. Did you know God sometimes speaks to us in a whisper and with a whistle?

GETTING ALONE

THERE'S SOMETHING ABOUT feeling hidden, when nobody knows your whereabouts. It's a camouflage, isn't it? Nowadays nothing is secret or sacred. Everybody wants to know your business. Everyone wants to know everything you're doing, every place you're going.

It's good to share your life with people, but sometimes we need to go away where nobody can find us. When I rendezvous, only those closest to me even know where I am.

SHUTTING OFF COMMUNICATION

IT'S OFTEN DIFFICULT for those in ministry to get away from

their phones. It takes a lot of planning to get away from phones, faxes and e-mail. In fact, we usually feel we need to take our phones with us, and our computers, too!

What in the world would happen if my phone no longer worked? It might be a God-send. In fact, I'm in a cottage that has no phone as I write this portion of the book. I encourage you to find a place you can go where there are no phones. Find a cottage or a camp—find a tent!

If you can't hide in your house, get somewhere that you can. It won't hurt you. To the contrary, it will do you a lot of good. Be ready to feel victorious when you come out.

TAKING A PRAYER PARTNER

I RECOMMEND GETTING away with one or two people. Sometimes you just need someone else to talk to. But pray for God's timing and perfect choice in this matter. It's very important to have God's choice for your prayer partner on a rendezvous.

Give yourself permission to put work aside. Be open to God's fresh insight. This time should be given for the purpose of washing, strengthening and clearing your thinking for whatever the Lord has directed.

BRING A BIBLE AND JOURNAL

YOU MAY WANT to bring some devotional materials with you and some books you've wanted to read for a long time. Take the Word of God out, and read it—don't just study it. Read His Word as a love letter to you from the Lord. Love letters are wonderful. Some people keep special letters they've received for years, stashed away in a box. After a while they take them out and read them again to encourage them, refresh their memory and help them relive the experience.

The Bible is a love letter to us from the Lord, and we need to take it out of the "box." Read it in a manner you haven't done for a long time—or perhaps never done before. Say to the Lord, "What is it You want to speak to me?" Savor His Word; enjoy it as if you're reading a marvelous romance novel.

Read the Bible as a powerful testimony book. Read it as an adventure book. Make some new discoveries as you read about history, and allow the unfolding of mysteries that come from the heart and mind of God. Take down some notes. Write in your journal. Be open for whatever the Lord might teach you.

The Bible is the Good Book. It will change your life. It is good food for your soul (Ps. 119:103). Just break out of your old patterns. Break the mold. Come away with your Beloved!

> For the word of God is living and active and sharper than any two-edged sword, and piercing as far as the division of soul and spirit, of both joints and marrow, and able to judge the thoughts and intentions of the heart. And there is no creature hidden from His sight, but all things are open and laid bare to the eyes of Him with whom we have to do. Since then we have a great high priest who has passed through the heavens, Jesus the Son of God, let us hold fast our confession. For we do not have a high priest who cannot sympathize with our weaknesses, but one who has been tempted in all things as we are, yet without sin. Let us therefore draw near with confidence to the throne of grace, that we may receive mercy and may find grace to help in time of need.
>
> —HEBREWS 4:12–16

This can be a special, secret time. A time of intrigue. A time of surprises. It's a time when you'll discover new things and sense a renewed curiosity in the Word of God. It's a time when you are seen by God and not by man, unless you've brought a friend. This is your special time when you reveal who you are to an audience of one—Jesus.

*P*resent your bodies a living and holy sacrifice, acceptable to God, which is your spiritual service of worship.

—Romans 12:1

8

Lessons Learned From a Consecrated One

$\mathcal{A}$ LIFE OF INTIMACY with God is a life of greater consecration and deeper devotion. To be consecrated is to give yourself completely to a purpose—God's purpose—no matter what it may be. Consecrated means we have laid our lives on the altar of God and have given up our own agendas, desires, goals and plans.

LESSONS LEARNED ABOUT CONSECRATION

SAMSON'S LIFE WAS consecrated to God by his parents before his birth. His life was given to him for God's divine plan of delivering Israel from the hand of their enemies, the Philistines.

The story of Samson, the consecrated one, provides a warning to all who desire to have a passionate love relationship with God. Will our passion be directed toward good, or will it be directed to the fulfillment of our own soul and flesh?

In the days of the judges, the Philistines were able to oppress Israel because of the evil in which Israel had become entangled. The Philistines represent the enemy, who constantly comes to batter us in an effort to take us over.

CONSECRATION: GOD'S CHOOSING

GOD WANTED TO deliver Israel from this oppression, and therefore He raised up Samson as deliverer—a man of passion. The Bible contains many stories of godly deliverers, both male and female, who came from different cultural backgrounds. God is no respecter of persons, and He chooses to use consecrated vessels who are willing to be used. God selected Samson to be a leader and deliverer for his nation. The oppression continued for many years, but God's chosen deliverer—who was not even born yet—was in the wings waiting for God's time.

It's comforting to realize that God knew ahead of time whom He wanted as the deliverer and from what lineage he would come. Before we were conceived in our mother's womb, the Lord chose the family into which we would be born. God knew whom we were going to be long before we were conceived. He had each one of us in His thoughts and considered what our special purpose would be. This is what's so wonderful about Samson's life. Long before he was in his mother's womb, God thought of him. And God had a purpose, plan and destiny for Samson to fulfill. Samson's life was very well thought out by God. And so it is with us: God knows what He wants of us and how He plans to bring it about. There are no mistakes.

CONSECRATION: GOD'S DESTINY

SAMSON WAS BORN into a family from the tribe of Dan. *Dan*

means "judge." God had commissioned the tribe of Dan to judge or rule over His people and subdue His enemies by His power.

The future destiny of the descendants of Dan was prophesied by Jacob. Scripture says, "Dan shall judge his people, as one of the tribes of Israel. Dan shall be a serpent in the way, a horned snake in the path, that bites the horse's heels, so that his rider falls backward" (Gen. 49:16–17).

So Samson was destined for leadership and to make his enemies fall backward as a mighty warrior. It was no mistake. Dan's tribe was destined to contend with the foes of Israel. Samson was destined to be "wise as a serpent and harmless as a dove" (Matt. 10:16). He was supposed to be wise and cunning, yet separated unto God.

CONSECRATION: GOD'S HERITAGE

SAMSON'S FATHER'S NAME was Manoah. The name *Manoah* means "rest and quiet." I believe that rest and quiet were part of Samson's heritage. Manoah is depicted as a God-fearing man who believed in prayer. The Lord chose Manoah and Samson's mother to be the guardians of His chosen deliverer. The parents that God chose for Samson were, I believe, prayer warriors. If Samson were living in our modern day, he would be considered a spiritual warfare strategist and great judge.

Samson came from a family that was involved in prayer and open to supernatural visitations.

> Now therefore, be careful not to drink wine or strong drink, nor eat any unclean thing. For behold, you shall conceive and give birth to a son, and no razor shall come upon his head, for the boy shall be a Nazirite to God from the womb; and he shall begin to deliver

Israel from the hands of the Philistines.

—JUDGES 13:4–5

Herein is the promise and the prophetic word that was spoken into Samson's mother's heart, giving her the faith to believe God to conceive. How many times we need to hear a prophetic word from God or a promise from the Lord through one of His messengers, assuring us that He is going to fulfill something that is empty in our lives. That's what He was doing here for Samson's mother. She was barren, and in those days, barrenness was a stigma.

What's wonderful is that she got direction from the Lord, through the angel, as to what to do. He told her how to help her child fulfill his destiny as a Nazirite—one called by God.

There is only so much you can do for your children, and the rest is between God and them. As I look at Samson's parents, I believe they gave him the best start he could have had. They dedicated, or consecrated, Samson to the Lord. His mother received the word from the Lord through an angel that he was to be a Nazirite, consecrated to God for a special purpose. The angel instructed what the Nazirite vows were to be, and Samson's mother followed these instructions.

CONSECRATION: THE NAZIRITE CALL

A NAZIRITE COULD be a man or a woman. In spiritual service, it doesn't matter what your gender is; God has called all of His people to be separated and consecrated unto Him.

There is neither Jew nor Greek, there is neither slave nor free man, there is neither male nor female; for you are all one in Christ Jesus. And if you belong to Christ, then you are Abraham's offspring, heirs according to promise.

—GALATIANS 3:28–29

The Nazirite didn't have to be a priest, hold a high office or be a judge or ruler. A Nazirite could be an everyday person.

The Nazirite did not have to be hidden away all the time like a monk but could mix with society. A Nazirite could live life in total freedom with people of the world and yet remain consecrated to God. I marvel at this fact, because it's only by the grace of God that any of us can live in this world and remain set apart to Him.

The three young Hebrew men in the Book of Daniel—Shadrach, Meshach and Abednego—experienced this. They were literally able to go through the fire and come out unsinged. This is the kind of consecrated life to which God is calling His people in this day and hour. With His grace, we will be able to do just that. Like the three young Hebrews, we should be able to walk through the fires of this world and come out without the smell of smoke on our clothing. We should be living out that separation so that we will be unscathed in the midst of it all. This was the prophetic word spoken over Samson, and he had the ability, through God, to do it.

CONSECRATION: ABSTAINING FROM THE WORLD'S WINE

A NAZIRITE HAD to fulfill three requirements for consecration: abstaining from wine and strong drink; never cutting the hair; and staying free from death and impurities. (See Judges 13:5; Numbers 6:2–21.) Samson and other Nazirites were to find their satisfaction in the presence of God, not wine.

I believe the abstinence from wine signifies the consecrated person's commitment to find satisfaction from the wine of the Holy Spirit. Samson's intoxication was to have been found in the presence of God. From a worldly viewpoint, wine and strong drink are considered to provide certain benefits to the drinker. These same benefits, including relaxation, euphoria and social communion, are to be sought and found in the Spirit of God by the one who is consecrated to Him.

> Wine is a mocker, strong drink a brawler, and whoever is intoxicated by it is not wise.
> —PROVERBS 20:1

People who get intoxicated with wine and strong drink end up becoming a mockery. They end up mocking God and the things of God. They laugh at things that are holy. Strong drink also stirs up anger and all the things that a consecrated one doesn't want to have stirred up inside.

CONSECRATION: DEVOTED FOR LIFE

THE UNCUT HAIR was a reminder of Samson's vows. Long hair was symbolic of a covering, and the length of the hair was to be a testimony of the length of the vow. Samson was a perpetual Nazirite from his mother's womb. Until death he was consecrated to the Lord; therefore he was never to cut his hair. Some took a short vow. If a Nazirite cut his hair, the vow would be completed, and the hair was to be burned with his sacrifice because it represented his vow. He was not allowed to use the hair for anything else because it was considered to be holy.

Scripture offers several figurative uses of hair. Hair represents marksmanship, such as missing a target by a "hair breadth" (Judg. 20:16). Hair sometimes represents safety (1 Sam. 14:45). Hair represents age or dignity in the Bible (Lev. 19:32; Prov. 16:31). It is a mark of beauty (1 Cor. 11:15). Sometimes it is a symbol of pride (1 Tim. 2:9). So for those who took a Nazirite vow, whether a man or a woman, the length of the hair was very significant.

CONSECRATION: FREE FROM
DEATH AND IMPURITY

THE THIRD REQUIREMENT was to stay undefiled from death and impurities. This is very significant because those who are consecrated to the Lord should walk holy and righteous before Him. We are in the world but not of it (John 17:14–15).

It was prophesied over Samson that he was to live his entire life free from the defilement of death, which represented sin. This was the intended destiny of Samson's life. But just because something is prophesied over you and promised to you doesn't automatically mean it's going to be fulfilled in your life. Each one of us has a part to play in the fulfillment of our destiny. It is required of each one of us that we obey in order to fulfill the promise of our destiny.

As consecrated believers, God requires that we stay away from the things of death and impurity. In the story of Samson these things are used to represent the deeds of darkness and unrighteousness. Consecrated believers must live holy lives.

CONSECRATION: THE POWER OF THE TONGUE

ONE WAY IN which consecrated believers must reject the power of death is to tame the tongue. The Bible says that the power of life and death resides in the tongue (Prov. 18:21). Our words can bring life, and our words can bring death. We are priests of the most high God. God has called us to be His prophetic people, and as such we should speak blessings over His people. We should speak goodness and life into people's lives. It's a shame that we sometimes speak curses and steal hope when we fail to speak encouragement and life into people. Using the power of the tongue in a godly way is a tremendous responsibility.

Numbers 6:8 says, "All the days of his separation he is holy to the LORD." This is one of the declarations over Nazirites, and the same should hold true for us. As long as they were Nazirites, they were to be holy to the Lord. When we received Christ, we began our separated life. This is God's call for us as it was to Samson.

CONSECRATION: THE GUARDED LIFE

Now therefore, be careful not to drink wine or strong drink, nor eat any unclean thing.

—JUDGES 13:4

It's interesting that the New American Standard Bible says *be careful,* which means "to guard." It's the same word that means to put a hedge of protection around, as of thorns. The angel was speaking to Samson's mother, cautioning her about the seriousness of her son's calling. Whatever she did would affect him physically and spiritually.

We must also guard ourselves. *Guard* is a term used in relation to spiritual warfare. We are to guard what we do and how we do it, because our lives are producing something. Samson's mother was going to produce a child who would be marked by her influence. She had to be extremely careful to do what was right, because this child was chosen by God for His purposes. Whatever she ate or drank would have passed through into Samson's blood system and perhaps created an appetite in him for the very things he was called to resist.

Samson's parents did everything they were required to do. The responsibility for fulfilling the calling would be Samson's at a later date. He would have significant choices to make that would affect an entire nation. He could never blame his parents for his failure.

Our calling and consecration is our responsibility. No one else can be blamed for our disobedience. When God calls us to perform a purpose, He equips us for success.

CONSECRATION: A SUPERNATURAL VISITATION

SAMSON'S MOTHER HAD a spiritual encounter, and later his father had one as well. After learning of his wife's experience, Manoah prayed.

> Then Manoah entreated the LORD and said, "O Lord, please let the man of God whom Thou hast sent come to us again that he may teach us what to do for the boy who is to be born."
>
> —JUDGES 13:8

This passage reveals Samson's godly heritage, passed down from his father and mother. *Entreat* is another word for pray. It is *athar* in Hebrew, which means "to burn incense in worship, i.e. intercede and also reciprocating, listening to prayer." Entreating the Lord is one form of petition, but it is a petition given with a worshipful heart. In other words, it's intercession riding on the wings of worship. It's prayer carrying a fragrance of intimate fellowship with God. Samson's heritage provided him with a knowledge of how to worship God in prayer. This Nazirite's relationship with the Lord was to be a sweet incense to God.

CONSECRATION: MAKING FATHERS AND MOTHERS IN ISRAEL

WHEN SAMSON'S PARENTS asked God to "teach us what to do," they revealed their character. This word for teach, *yara*, means "to flow as water (i.e. to rain). Translated to lay or throw, (especially an arrow, i.e. to shoot); figuratively to point out as if aiming the finger), to teach."

Manoah wanted to know what he needed to do to help his son realize his calling. Manoah told God he needed teaching that would flow as water—he knew he had a lot to learn. He needed God to teach him continually in order to get his son going in the right direction. His son could be like an arrow. Psalm 127:4 speaks about children being like arrows in the hand of a warrior. Samson seemed destined to have many of the same qualities as his father: He was to be a person of peace and rest, of prayer and worship and one who asks for help to hit the mark.

The Lord is calling His people to be mothers and fathers in Israel. We're living in an apostolic time when God is calling us to be the model. He is calling us to be the Nazirites and the parents of Nazirites. We need to be able to go into any given situation and walk upright before the Lord and before all the people of the world so they'll know who we are in Christ.

We'll have a symbol. It won't be long hair—the symbol of our consecration to God will be the glory covering our heads, our minds and our thinking. Once people are drawn to us through Christ, we'll be able to help them fulfill their destiny. The Lord calls us to reproduce ourselves and to be examples, as Manoah was. But we will have to trust God and give them to Him, for they too need to make their own decisions.

CONSECRATION: LISTENING
AND THE SABBATH REST

> God listened to the voice of Manoah; and the angel of
> God came again to the woman as she was sitting in the
> field, but Manoah her husband was not with her.
>
> —JUDGES 13:9

When Samson's mother and father prayed, God listened. They had the ear of God. The Hebrew word for hear or listen is *shama*. It means "to hear intelligently (often with implication of getting the attention, obedience; cause to tell)." God was not just listening to Manoah's words; He was listening to Manoah's heart. That's what prayer is. More than the words we say, prayer is the motivation of our hearts. It is the deepest expressions of our inner man.

I believe God listened to Manoah because Manoah had entered into the Sabbath rest. This is a place where the flesh is silent and the spirit-man speaks. Samson was called to go against the enemies of Israel, and in the midst of the turmoil of warfare he was to be a godly example.

In verse 9, God answered Manoah's entreaty. However, the angel doesn't return to Manoah. Instead he goes to the one to whom the word of prophecy was first given: Samson's mother. She was to carry out this prophetic word of promise. Manoah's wife was the bearer of this prophet of God. It was ultimately her responsibility to make sure she did all the things required, because she was the one who was to give birth.

CONSECRATION: GUARDING THE PURPOSE OF GOD

So the woman ran quickly and told her husband, "Behold, the man who came the other day has appeared to me." Then Manoah arose and followed his wife, and when he came to the man he said to him, "Are you the man who spoke to the woman?" And he said, "I am." And Manoah said, "Now when your words come to pass, what shall be the boy's mode of life and his vocation?" So the angel of the LORD said to Manoah, "Let the woman pay attention to all that I said."

—JUDGES 13:10–13

Those who have a responsibility to guard a word of destiny from God are those who will receive it. Others can help protect the word to a certain extent. But in the end no one else is responsible for the prophetic word spoken into our lives but us. No one else is responsible for the promises given into our lives, even though our moms, dads and friends in ministry may help us fulfill them.

Each one of us is our brother's keeper. However, what God has spoken to me individually, I have the responsibility and choice to do or not. Manoah was praying, and God came. The Lord answered him, but He went directly to the one who was going to carry the promise, the one who was responsible for the prophetic word, the one who was going to birth it into being.

In Judges 13:14, the angel repeated the requirements of a Nazirite. This demonstrates the graciousness of God as He reminds us of what we need to do. He knows our humanity. God knew that these two people were fallible and fragile. They were reminded of the requirements on more than one occasion to make sure they would do what was right according to the Lord.

CONSECRATION: A REVELATION OF JESUS

JUDGES 13:17 SAYS, "Manoah said to the angel of the LORD, 'What is your name, so that when your words come to pass, we may honor you?'" The angel did not want Manoah and his wife to focus on who delivered the word from God. Our focus is never to be on the person who gives us the prophetic word. Our focus must always remain on God.

The angel's assignment was to get the word to Manoah and his wife and to help them stay on target. Keep your focus; keep God in the center. It was very important that Samson's parents did this before the child was born.

> But the angel of the Lord said to him, "Why do you ask my name, seeing it is wonderful?"
>
> —Judges 13:18

This is so exciting! Let's examine this word *wonderful* closely. The messianic prophecy of Isaiah 9:6 uses the Hebrew word *peli,* meaning "wonderful." This suggests that the angel who appeared to Samson's parents may have been Jesus! This appearance is referred to as a "theophany"—a visible manifestation when God appears in another form. In this instance, Jesus appeared. This is what makes Samson's call so wonderful. His parents not only had a visitation from an angel of God, but possibly from Jesus Himself! Jesus' name is incomprehensible. He is wonderful and marvelous! "His name will be called Wonderful Counselor, Mighty God, Eternal Father, Prince of Peace" (Isa. 9:6).[1]

CONSECRATION: A CALL OF WORSHIP

> So Manoah took the young goat with the grain offering and offered it on the rock to the Lord, and He performed wonders while Manoah and his wife looked on. For it came about when the flame went up from the altar toward heaven, that the angel of the Lord ascended in the flame of the altar. When Manoah and his wife saw this, they fell on their faces to the ground. Now the angel of the Lord appeared no more to Manoah or his wife. Then Manoah knew that he was the angel of the Lord.
>
> —Judges 13:19–21

Once the prophetic word was received, Manoah and his wife worshiped at the altar. Instead of taking the goat to have a celebration for themselves, they gave it to the Lord in worship.

The whole emphasis in the beginning of Samson's life was consecration, preparation, worship and adoration. It wasn't partying. God performed wonders through the angel before Manoah and his wife's eyes. The angel never appeared again. God comes and visits us, but He doesn't always come back again the same way. Manoah and his wife were on their way to learning the ways of God.

Judges 13:22 says, "So Manoah said to his wife, 'We shall surely die, for we have seen God.'" Manoah had progressed from seeing a stranger, or a man, to recognizing this individual as an angel of the Lord, to a final realization that he and his wife were experiencing a revelation of God Himself. I call this a *progressive revelation*. An intimate relationship with God is developed over a process of time.

God reveals Himself to us in a progressive manner as we sincerely seek Him. There's always progression—always something more that God desires to reveal to us. During the worship time at the altar, Samson's parents' eyes were opened to see the fuller revelation of God appearing to them. Their discernment improved as they became more focused on God. Ultimately, the result of this progressive revelation was that they saw God. This is the cry of many hearts today. We want to see Jesus.

The life of Samson is not just a nice Sunday school story for kids. God's Word is powerfully relevant, with life lessons revealed in the lives of the saints and preserved for us to grow by.

In Judges 13:19 we see the angel of the Lord ascending to heaven in the flames of the altar while Manoah and his wife fall on their faces in an act of worship and fear of God. Once again we are permitted to witness godly attributes in this couple. They are humble worshipers whose reverence for God would be passed down to their son. As the angel of the Lord arises in the flames of the altar, we know that God has accepted the godly sacrifice of this couple.

POWER IS THE FRUIT OF A CONSECRATED LIFE

But his wife said to him, "If the LORD had desired to
kill us, He would not have accepted a burnt offering
and a grain offering from our hands, nor would He
have shown us all these things, nor would He have let
us hear things like this at this time." Then the woman
gave birth to a son and named him Samson; and the
child grew up and the LORD blessed him.
—JUDGES 13:23–24

God had waited forty years to send a deliverer to Israel.
When He sent this deliverer, it was at the right time and
season—not just for the people of Israel, but for Manoah
and his wife, too. It was God's time to give them the
guardianship of Samson and the prophetic word. Manoah
and his wife could be trusted.

Samson's parents chose his name, which meant "sunlike,
sunny, little sun." It also meant "destroyer." His name suggests that this child was full of energy and light. And he was
filled with God's power.

CONSECRATION: THE POWER
TO PULL DOWN STRONGHOLDS

THE WORD *DESTROYER* means to "pull down and to tear to
pieces." It means to "ruin, to bring to nought, to spoil completely." Samson was born into this world with purpose. He
was consecrated and called to destroy the works of darkness.

This is exactly what God has called us to do in this spiritually dark hour. God is calling us to be a people so full of light
that darkness is dispelled by our very presence. Strongholds
should crumple by our presence. It's only as we grow intimate

with God and live our lives in His presence that we will become anointed to such an extent.

Samson's name revealed his calling—the calling of a consecrated believer. Samson's name also means to "make useless." The anointing that comes as a result of our consecration will make Satan and all his cohorts useless. We are to make all of his lies, deceptions and plots useless.

Samson was a man of spiritual strength and zeal, but he was also a man of pride and presumption, which led in part to his downfall. Nevertheless, he is listed in the faith hall of fame (Heb. 11:32).

CONSECRATION: A LIFE OF BLESSING

SPECIAL BLESSING FOLLOWS special consecration. God is faithful to His promises and will bless us even when we don't bless Him. God's blessings hovered mightily upon Samson because of his consecration. Samson faltered in his humanness, but the blessings of God never faltered.

The Hebrew word for bless is *barak.* It means "to kneel," and by implication to bless God as an act of adoration; vice versa, to bless man as a benefactor. It also means "to congratulate, to praise, to salute." God came down and blessed Samson.

> And the child grew up and the LORD blessed him. And the Spirit of the LORD began to stir him in Mahaneh-dan, between Zorah and Eshtaol.
> —JUDGES 13:24–25

The Holy Spirit moved upon the Old Testament prophets in different ways. But today, He lives, moves and has His being in us. He abides in us, and the anointing is within us whether we know it or not.

Today the Holy Spirit stirs many, not just one or two as in Samson's time. If Samson were in today's church, I believe he would not be only a spiritual warfare strategist but also a Holy Spirit-stirred man of God. Samson's life of special consecration led to a life of deep anointing, gifting and empowerment.

CONSECRATION: A LIFE OF GREAT MANIFESTED POWER

SAMSON EXPERIENCED CHARISMATIC revival as a result of consecration. Subsequently, he walked in great power with all the manifestations of the Holy Spirit operating in him.

The term *Spirit of God* comes from the Hebrew word *ruwach.* It means "wind; by resemblance, breath, i.e. a sensible (or even violent) exhalation." It also can mean life, and even anger.

The *ruwach* of God, or the presence of God, was manifested to Samson in a unique way because of his consecration. It was a violent manifestation. Some of us have experienced the wind of God in a similar way. Samson shook when the wind of God came upon him. He experienced a wild manifestation, like the wind of a tornado or a tempest.

I believe that as the Spirit of the Lord rushed upon Samson, he experienced a manifestation similar to those experienced during recent outpourings of the Holy Spirit throughout the United States and around the world. I don't believe it was "violent" in a negative sense, just overwhelmingly powerful. This manifestation of the Spirit that Samson experienced was a glorious display of the pleasure and power of God's presence. It was an outward show of an inward work of the holy power of the Lord.

CONSECRATION: LEARNING
THE WAYS OF GOD'S SPIRIT

WHEN SAMSON GREW to a place of maturity, the promises and prophetic words spoken over his life began to be fulfilled. The first great manifestation of power was the rushing wind of the Holy Spirit upon his life. The Spirit of the Lord, the *ruwach,* came upon him, stirring him and shaking him to the core of his being. Samson was given a blast of the breath of God. He had been taught about God by his parents through their witness and example. Now God came into Samson's life to reveal His presence and power in an intimate way. God didn't come in just a little bit—God came in a big way!

At this point Samson's understanding of the ways of God's Spirit changed from childhood knowledge into the mature knowledge of manhood. Samson grew to a place of transformation, of understanding the different movings of God. Samson had been roused. The one who had been called sunlike was being enlightened by the power of the Holy Spirit.

What happened to Samson was not a passive experience. Encounters with the Lord are not always passive. Sometimes there's a stillness, a silence, which I have discussed at length in this book. But other times are marked by a dynamic and glorious encounter with the living God. Samson was awakened with "fervor." He was consumed with the zeal of God.

CONSECRATION: EMPOWERMENT
AND DIRECTION FOR MINISTRY

And the Spirit of the LORD began to stir him in Mahaneh-dan.

—JUDGES 13:25

The tribe of Dan camped in Mahaneh-dan. It was here that the Holy Spirit first moved upon Samson, and it was here that he was buried. Mahaneh-dan was the place of his life and death in the Holy Spirit.

Samson received that first stirring in the place known for his tribe. Mahaneh-dan was his home base. The gifts of the Holy Spirit were greatly stirred up in Samson. (See 2 Timothy 1:6: "And for this reason I remind you to kindle afresh the gift of God which is in you through the laying on of my hands.")

Samson's home base happened to be between Zorah and Eshtaol. Samson was born in Zorah. *Eshtaol* means "petition," and *Zorah* means "to stroke, strike or scourge." In most of the biblical references, these two towns are mentioned together. On one side of his home base was a place of prayer, or petition to God. On the other lay *Zorah,* which means stroke or scourge.

This is where God met Samson, and it's where God meets us—at our home base. God meets us where we are in order to take us to where He is. God meets us down where we live, with affliction on one side and the choice to petition Him in prayer on the other.

There's usually some catalyst that draws us to the Lord, something that makes us desire more of Him. Certain things seem to work together, leading us to petition God in a way that eventually brings down His power and presence, resulting in revival.

Between Eshtaol and Zorah, at Mahaneh-dan, the Spirit of God first stirred Samson to move against the Philistines. Not only did he have a personal empowerment from the Holy Spirit, but he also received direction from the Lord. With this empowerment Samson received the motivation to be the deliverer of Israel.

CONSECRATION: BROKEN VOWS

BEING CONSECRATED, OR given completely to Jesus Christ, is not a guarantee that we will never again be tempted. Jesus Himself was tempted, but He never sinned. (See Luke 4; Hebrews 2:1–18; 4:15.) Temptation abounds in the lives of all believers, especially those with a deep commitment to God. Our hearts are in constant danger of being drawn away from our first love. The hot flame of passionate love for Christ can easily wane. We must constantly be vigilant to guard the passion of our hearts.

After Samson's marvelous experience with God, he went down to Temnah where he saw and desired one of the daughters of the uncircumcised Philistines. Samson returned home and told his father and mother to get her for him to be his wife. His parents objected, questioning Samson's choice. They strongly encouraged him to choose one of their own family.

Samson's reply is found in Judges 14:3: "Get her for me, for she looks good to me." His parents did not realize that God was using Samson's own fleshly human desires—the lust of the flesh, the lust of the eyes and the pride of life—for God's benefit and for the benefit of the Israelites. (See 1 John 2:16.)

The Lord will even use our sinful tendencies to His own advantage. Samson's parents tried to steer him in the right direction, but to no avail.

> And behold, a young lion came roaring toward him. And the Spirit of the LORD came upon him mightily, so that he tore him as one tears a kid though he had nothing in his hand; but he did not tell his father or mother what he had done. So he went down and talked to the woman; and she looked good to

Samson. When he returned later to take her, he turned aside to look at the carcass of the lion; and behold, a swarm of bees and honey were in the body of the lion. So he scraped the honey into his hands and went on, eating as he went. When he came to his father and mother, he gave some to them and they ate it; but he did not tell them that he had scraped the honey out of the body of the lion.

—JUDGES 14:5–9

Samson showed a lack of integrity by not telling his parents that he scraped the honey out of the lion's carcass. He was breaking a vow when he tasted of death, and he drew his parents unknowingly into his own sin.

CONSECRATION: MAINTAINING GODLY RELATIONSHIPS

AFTER HIS FIRST major encounter with the Lord, Samson wanted something that looked good to him. In 2 Corinthians 6:14 Paul writes, "Do not be bound together with unbelievers; for what partnership have righteousness and lawlessness, or what fellowship has light with darkness?" The Bible counsels to marry only in the Lord. (See 1 Corinthians 7:39.) Samson disobeyed this important principle: Consecration requires that we maintain godly relationships.

Just because we have a wonderful encounter with the Holy Spirit doesn't mean we're going to do everything right. As soon as His manifested presence lifts from us, we still have choices to make with opportunities to sin. Trials usually follow great spiritual encounters, testing and revealing our true relationship. We look into the eyes of the Lord, and then He looks into ours, right down into our soul. Samson didn't heed his parents' warning. His second major experience in the Holy Spirit actually brought death into his relationship with his parents.

CONSECRATION: DRAWN AWAY BY WORLDLY WAYS

SAMSON WAS PRETTY popular, and not only with the women. It seems he could easily draw a crowd of peers around him, for thirty young men joined him at a feast he held.

He was an individual with great intelligence, wit and humor. He had many riddles to tell, and he seemed to be the life of the party. Everyone loved Samson. This became a snare that led to boastful pride. The Bible says, "Do not love the world, nor the things in the world. If anyone loves the world, the love of the Father is not in him. For all that is in the world, the lust of the flesh and the lust of the eyes and the boastful pride of life, is not from the Father, but is from the world. And the world is passing away, and also its lusts; but the one who does the will of God lives forever" (1 John 2:15–16).

Samson's example is a warning to those who want to walk intimately with the Lord and maintain a godly character. Samson's weaknesses can be in any of us who have been consecrated and set apart by God. Sometimes we're fooled by our anointing and gifting, and we mistake our anointing for proof of our character and maturity in Christ.

We see the pattern beginning here when Samson surrendered to his wife after she pressed him for seven days to tell her the answer to one of his riddles. She and her father were in danger of losing everything. But such shallow relationships are not for those who are in covenant with God. They can eventually bring a snare.

Then the Spirit of the LORD came upon him mightily,

and he went down to Ashkelon and killed thirty of them and took their spoil, and gave the changes of clothes to those who told the riddle. And his anger burned, and he went up to his father's house. But Samson's wife was given to his companion who had been his friend.

—JUDGES 14:19–20

Samson's anger was a reflection of his passionate nature, which needed to be redirected and submitted to God. Samson is recorded in the hall of faith in Hebrews, and he remained a Nazirite all the days of his life, with the Holy Spirit's power upon him. But this didn't change the nature of his character. That was Samson's responsibility—a responsibility at which he failed miserably. The anointing of God's power didn't keep all these calamities from happening to him, and it didn't assure him of a pure heart. Purity and godly character are always an individual's choice, no matter how gifted or anointed that person may be.

CONSECRATION: GUARDING THE HEART

GOD SPOKE TO me years ago and told me to guard the anointing, to guard what He gives to me and what I impart to others. Be very careful in how you handle the anointing.

The Lord warns the body of Christ to be careful and to wait for His timing. Just because I have a prophetic word doesn't mean I have to declare it. Just because I have an anointing operating in me doesn't mean I have to give it away or minister to someone. All that I have and know doesn't have to be revealed. Learn to be selective about how you operate in the Holy Spirit's gifting. Is God receiving the glory? Is it God's timing? Sometimes the Spirit of God comes upon us for the future, not necessarily for an immediate act to execute. Sometimes the unction of the Holy Spirit comes upon us to store up power within our inner man in preparation for a later time. Sometimes He comes upon us just to bless us.

CONSECRATION: MAINTAIN AN INTIMATE RELATIONSHIP WITH GOD

THE BIBLE RECORDS three major encounters with the Holy Spirit in Samson's life. Despite his great calling and empowerment, it doesn't appear that Samson spent much time in prayer and worship or in maintaining an intimate relationship with the Lord.

Many people have incredible encounters with the Holy Spirit and go right from one experience to the next without ever developing an intimate relationship with the Lord. They do not become still before Him, they do not wait for His presence and consequently they do not hear from Him in a continual way.

The story of Samson provides a powerful lesson on the pitfalls of walking in the power and calling of a consecrated life. The Bible shows several areas in which Samson missed it, eventually leading to his downfall.

USING THE ANOINTING FOR SELFISH GAIN

SAMSON USED GOD'S power for his own pleasure and gain each time the Spirit came upon him. A great responsibility goes in tandem with being a carrier of God's gifts and blessed Holy Spirit.

When Samson didn't get an immediate rebuke from God for his selfish behavior, he developed a false sense of security. He began to feel that he could get away with much.

When a supernatural touch comes upon our lives, we can begin to feel that our life is not governed by the same rules that apply to others. This is self-delusion. The more blessed we are with spiritual gifts, the more accountable we are to walk in those gifts in a godly way.

Samson received correction quickly from his parents, but he chose to ignore it. God kept quiet. And there's no indication that Samson said anything to God following these three major encounters. Samson set himself up for failure, and God gave him the space to experience it. Samson was being drawn into a trap by his own sinful nature.

If entanglement with sin is so easy to fall into, what does the believer do? How can we be assured of success in our determination to live a consecrated life? The answer is found in Scripture:

> Therefore, since we have so great a cloud of witnesses surrounding us, let us also lay aside every encumbrance, and the sin which so easily entangles us, and let us run with endurance the race that is set before us, fixing our eyes on Jesus, the author and perfecter of faith, who for the joy set before Him endured the cross, despising the shame, and has sat down at the right hand of the throne of God. For consider Him who has endured such hostility by sinners against Himself, so that you will not grow weary and lose heart. You have not yet resisted to the point of shedding blood in your striving against sin; and you have forgotten the exhortation which is addressed to you as sons, "My son, do not regard lightly the discipline of the Lord, nor faint when you are reproved by Him; for those whom the Lord loves He disciplines, and He scourges every son whom He receives."
>
> —Hebrews 12:1–6

Always choose to receive the Lord's correction. Correction is one of God's way of expressing His deep love and affection for us. We must never harden our hearts when we receive correction through the words of others or through the Word of God. God offers a path for success with all the resources we need to triumph, but success in the Spirit is always our choice.

TOTAL SURRENDER

IT'S A SHAME that Samson didn't heed the correction sent by God through his parents. He no doubt closed his ears to the promptings of the Holy Spirit. Samson had been well trained in the requirements of his devoted life, but he chose to break each and every vow of his consecration.

When he broke the first vow and seemed to get away with it, his heart only grew harder. We look at Samson and wonder how he could have been so blind as not to see through Delilah's trap. He chose blindness each time he rejected his vows and pursued worldly pleasure. His self-imposed spiritual blindness eventually resulted in physical blindness when the Philistines gouged out his eyes and made him an object of scorn.

Samson was seduced by the world and couldn't see through its evil motives until it was too late. In his physical blindness, captured and broken by the Philistines, he finally became aware of the true nature of his enemies, whose favor he once sought.

He was a man given to his own passion and anger. Although consecrated to God, Samson never really yielded his will to the Lord. He had given enough of himself to God that the Spirit of God moved upon him, but he wasn't completely given over to God. What we see in Samson is what we see today with many men of God in high places who have been seduced by sexual lust and greed. The Bible warns us to flee youthful lust. We must take heed to Samson's example. It's not enough to give "just enough" of ourselves to God. We must give ourselves completely to Him.

OPERATING IN GIFTS WITHOUT INTIMACY

SAMSON EXERCISED STRENGTH, power and gifts without intimacy. He exercised authority with God because of who he was—because of his calling, appointing and anointing. He had a relationship with God but not an intimate relationship. His prayers, though small, were heard and answered. He captured the city and carried the gates off on his shoulders. He had a greater passion for women than for God. He was a man of faith but not of intimacy.

Samson began to let Delilah fill the need for intimacy in his life. She demanded the throne room and innermost chambers of his heart. She wanted the place that should have been reserved only for God. She wanted his body, soul and spirit. She wanted his heart because she already had his mind. Delilah represents the world, which cannot be content with part of our hearts but forever demands more until it owns all.

The enemy's strategy is to get our minds off good and pure things. The mind is the battlefield. If Satan can shift our focus from God and pull our thoughts toward the things of this world and the flesh, eventually he can get our inner chamber that is to be reserved for the Lord. It was only a matter of time before Delilah knew all that was in Samson's heart: his secrets, his sacred covenant relationship with God. When you're set apart for the Lord, your inner vulnerability, or nakedness, belongs to God. Delilah wanted Samson's inner man—his marriage, if you will, with his God.

God foreordained Samson to have a precious relationship with the Lord, but Delilah's satanic assignment kept that from happening. Your fellowship with God is very important to

Him. It hurts Him deeply when men and women reject Jesus Christ. God created us and gave us life in order to live in wonderful fellowship with our Creator. His heart longs for us with a love that we will never fully comprehend.

LOVING THE GIFT, NOT THE GIVER

PEOPLE TEND TO look at the gifts, not at the Giver of those gifts. Samson had powerful spiritual gifts operating in his life. He walked in a divine calling and anointing, and he had great authority. He was a judge and a Nazirite, and the people lived in peace for twenty years under his reign. God answered his prayers mightily.

Just because your prayers are answered doesn't mean you're right with God. Just because you walk in authority doesn't mean you have it all together. It is only by God's grace that we walk in the gifts of the Holy Spirit.

If we experience powerful results from our prayers, it's not proof that we are good or that we're doing everything correctly. Scripture says if we hold iniquity in our hearts, God won't hear us. Although some people speak the name of Jesus or command demonic spirits to leave, that still doesn't indicate they have an intimate walk with God.

TAKING GOD'S GRACE LIGHTLY

TOO OFTEN WE break our promises, but God never breaks His. When we fall short and realize just how faithful He is, it causes us to desire greater intimacy with the Lord.

We can be fooled by looking at those who operate with great spiritual strength and power. When we begin to judge people by their gifts, we fall into error. Samson is a good example of one who exercised the power of God but abused the privileges of his calling. The Spirit of God came upon him mightily and set him apart from other people. But Samson made wrong choices. He got his own way for a time, and it probably looked to him and those around him that God didn't mind the bad choices he'd made. Unfortunately, by abusing the power and privilege of his office, he lay a snare for himself that eventually caught up with him.

Instead of walking in the anointing with a holy reverence, Samson took the power of God lightly. I see the body of Christ acting in a similar way, taking lightly the grace of God. It takes a lot more to attain a rich walk with God than it does to develop in the power gifts. It takes much more to develop godly character than to walk in spiritual gifts. Samson was a man who displayed power but failed in his walk with God.

THE CHARACTER OF GOD

THE ONLY VISIBLE sign of an intimate walk with the Lord is character. It's our character that truly displays the person of God to a lost and dying world.

Godly character, the genuine love of Jesus Christ, is the true fruit of our relationship with the Lord. I've seen many men and women of God who moved with great authority, commanding great miracles. But only God knows who each individual is before the throne of the Father.

Samson's life stands as a great warning to all who would know God in a deeper dimension. Take the lessons of this hero of faith to heart, and never lose sight of the purpose for our spirituality: to know the love of God and to reveal that love to others.

The harvest is plentiful,
but the workers are few.
Therefore beseech the Lord
of the harvest to send out
workers into His harvest.

—Matthew 9:37–38

9

I Love the Lord
of the Harvest

J ESUS CHRIST IS called the Lord of the harvest. Many believe that we are living in the time that the Bible refers to as the "great harvest." This is a time when Jesus Christ, the Lord of the Harvest, will manifest His presence in the earth in order to gather souls into His kingdom in great numbers.

MEDITATIONS OF THE GREAT HARVEST OF GOD

TO COMPLETE MY prayer journey I decided to visit a modern-day harvest to observe and meditate so that God could speak to my spirit about the great harvest of souls He's about to bring upon the earth.

As I look out at the harvest fields of hay through the window of the guest cabin in Camano Island, I envision Jesus Christ in heaven, looking at the human fields of harvest on earth. He sees every needy soul who would respond to the gospel if given the opportunity. He also sees every soul who has rejected His offer of salvation when they were given the opportunity. He sees every longing of each human soul, filled with questions that He could so easily answer. What does He see as He looks out at the fields that are white for harvest? If they were only hungry enough and would only ask, He would answer them. If we would go and tell them, they would know and understand.

> Do you not say, "There are yet four months, and then comes the harvest?" Behold I say to you, lift up your eyes, and look on the fields, that they are white for harvest.
> —JOHN 4:35

We need to see with the eyes of Jesus, to see the harvest as He sees it. Some of us are out in the harvest fields, yet we don't realize we're out there. We don't pay any attention to the places we go. We don't pay attention to the fact that there are people who need to know Christ when we go into the marketplace. We're not sensitized to it. We just go out more or less with blinders on. We just go and do what we need to do for ourselves, then we forget about praying for those among whom we've walked. We forget about asking the Holy Spirit to use us and show us what to do or say. We forget to ask Him to show us if we need to comfort someone, pray for someone, be kind or smile at someone, bless someone or listen to someone as Jesus would have done.

Multitudes are out there ready to be harvested if only we would be willing to walk among people who are different from ourselves. Think how many people we could win for the kingdom of God if we'd be willing to go into places that may feel uncomfortable to us. We must be willing to strike up conversation with those who are different from us. We need to respond with the compassion of Christ to their hurts and pain.

HE SENT THEM OUT TO LOVE WITH HIS LOVE

The love of God is shed abroad in our hearts by the Holy Ghost which is given unto us.

—ROMANS 5:5, KJV

I love the Lord of the harvest. And if I love the Lord of the harvest, I love what He loves—and He loves the harvest. That is every man, woman and child from every walk of life and nationality—every color, kindred, tribe, tongue and nation. (See Matthew 26:75; Luke 19:41; John 11:35.) The love of Christ is in my being. Jesus was moved with compassion and weeping. He wept over Lazarus and over the city of Jerusalem. Oh, how He loved the city, how He loved Israel, how He loved the Jews! How He loves all people! God wants us to look out and see what He sees—to see all the people whom He created and to love them.

Do you look at the sea of humanity and see what Jesus saw? Loving the needy people of the world is the reason Jesus sent out the seventy disciples. He sent out workers to save and heal a sick and dying world, a world of people for whom He died.

Now after this the Lord appointed seventy others, and sent them two and two ahead of Him to every city and place where He Himself was going to come. And He was saying to them, "The harvest is plentiful, but the laborers are few; therefore beseech the Lord of the harvest to send out laborers into His harvest. Go your ways; behold, I send you out as lambs in the midst of wolves. Carry no purse, no bag, no shoes; and greet no one on the way. And whatever house you enter, first say, 'Peace be to this house.' And if a man of peace is there, your peace will rest upon him; but if not, it will return to you. And stay in that house, eating and drinking what they give you; for the laborer is worthy of his wages. Do not keep moving from house to house. And whatever city you enter, and they receive you, eat what is set before you; and heal those in it who are sick, and say to them, 'The kingdom of God has come near to you.' But whatever city you enter and they do not receive you, go out into its streets and say, 'Even the dust of your city which clings to our feet, we wipe off in protest against you; yet be sure of this, that the kingdom of God has come near.' And I say to you, it will be more tolerable in that day for Sodom, than for that city."

—LUKE 10:1–12

HE SENT THEM INTO
THE HARVEST TWO BY TWO

WHEN JESUS SENT out the seventy, He sent them two by two. There's a time for solitude and setting ourselves apart. But there's also a time when we cannot just be alone with Him. We must go out two by two. Sometimes the Lord wants us alone in the prayer closet, and at other times He wants us out there in the fields.

Years ago the Lord told me He had called me into the prayer closet with Him for the purpose of going out to the people with His love. He wants us out there laboring in the particular field He has chosen for us to bring in the harvest. We need to be instant in season and out (2 Tim. 4:2). We need to be willing to give an account for the things we believe (1 Pet. 3:15). Sometimes we may do that without the help of others. On those occasions the Holy Spirit is our partner.

When we're alone with Him in the secret place, we learn that He is our partner. We learn much about abiding in Jesus. We learn that we can't do anything alone (John 15:5). When He sends us out two by two, He wants us to partner with another. We may partner with another in prayer, praying that He would save many souls and send other workers to help. May His kingdom come on earth as it is in heaven.

Being sent out two by two can also represent joining in vision and purpose with others in the body of Christ. Jesus prayed for believers to experience a unity of heart and mind—a oneness. (See John 17.) He cried out to the Father in the final days before His death, asking that we would operate as one in heart and mind so that others would know we were His disciples by our love.

HE SENT THEM TO PREPARE THE WAY

WHEN JESUS SENT out the seventy to every city and place that He Himself planned to visit, they were to prepare the way for the Master's visitation. Today we are still to go out two by two, linked arm in arm together. If we're united in spiritual intimacy with God, we will find that we also share an intimacy with others in the body of Christ. A fruit of our intimacy with God is learning how to relate to all of God's people, joining arms and hands and coming together to do the work of the ministry.

The Bible tells us to ask God for laborers for the harvest. Luke 10:2 says, "Beseech the Lord of the harvest to send out laborers into His harvest." *Beseech* means "to beg, to petition: to pray (to), and to make request." This word *beg* speaks of an attitude of humility, servanthood and supplication. Sometimes as we pray in the Holy Spirit there's a pleading with God, a requesting that adamantly cries out for souls. But it should always be made by one who is humble before God.

HE SENT THEM AS LAMBS AMONG WOLVES

"BEHOLD, I SEND you out as sheep in the midst of wolves, therefore be shrewd as serpents, and innocent as doves" (Matt. 10:16). The King James Version says, "Be ye therefore wise as serpents, and harmless as doves." In this way God molds our character in the midst of wolves. He does a work in our inmost being. While we're hidden away in relationship with Him, He works on us, and we become like doves. He works on our personality and character. "Iron sharpens iron, so one sharpens another" (Prov. 27:17).

When we are sharpened by one another, we help each other become wonderful instruments for God's purposes. We all are affecting each others' lives in ways that make us more pleasing, tender and sensitive. We become more like doves. Being with Jesus helps us to become innocent and pure. We also become harmless lambs. The fruit of intimacy with Jesus that grows ever deeper is that we become harmless and sensitive to other people—especially those who are most unlike us.

Nevertheless, as our characters are molded into a godly gentleness, a strength is also built into us that enables us to deal with the wolves. We become stronger in Him and yet more sensitive at the same time. It's quite a paradox to grow strong, cunning and wise, and at the same time to be innocent, harmless and pure. This is the fruit of an intimate relationship with Christ.

The Lord helps us to discern when others are being motivated by the enemy. When you see the enemy trying to come in and stop the work of God, you deal with him in an aggressive way, yet you always deal with people tenderly. You're able to distinguish the difference because you know that we do not fight against flesh and blood. We're fighting against the enemy and all the principalities and rulers of darkness. (See Ephesians 6:12.) That's what the Bible means when it says we are sent out to the harvest as lambs in the midst of wolves.

HE SENT THEM FOR A SINGLE-MINDED PURPOSE

WHEN JESUS SENT out the laborers into the harvest fields He told them to "carry no purse, no bag, no shoes; and greet no one on the way" (Luke 10:4).

When God sends us out from our prayer closet, He commissions us—He gives us an assignment. These heavenly orders are to be carried out with a single heart and a single mind. Never allow the enemy to pull you away or distract you from God's purposes. Too often those who are sent become sidetracked by distractions. These distractions can be snares laid by the devil to stop you from achieving your purpose of bringing souls into the kingdom.

By refusing to speak about our assignments to others, by refusing to turn aside to the plans of others, we are guarding the purpose of God. His orders, placed in our hearts by the Holy Spirit during prayer, carry with them the authority and power from heaven to save souls. A wise servant carefully guards those plans, focusing upon the divine purpose of God until all has been accomplished.

"And whatever house you enter, first say, 'Peace be to this house'" (Luke 10:5). Tremendous peace and rest are found in the Lord. When we are in the presence of the Prince of peace and then go to spend time with others, we bring peace. We bring peace to the harvest fields, to the troubled world.

HE SENT THEM TO COMPEL THE LOST TO COME IN

And the master said to the slave, "Go out into the

highways and along the hedges, and compel them to come in, that my house may be filled."

—LUKE 14:23

We must be prepared to go out to the highways and byways and compel them to come in by our love and peace—not with our words only. We can compel them to come in only at the level of zeal we have in our own beings. The degree to which we are stirred and motivated by God Himself is the degree to which we will go out and compel them to come in.

How does this happen? It comes only through a relationship with Him. When we compel them to come in, it will not be with hitting them over the head with a Bible. It will not be with anger and brashness. Instead, we will be men and women of peace. Jesus told His disciples that if a man of peace is there, their peace would rest upon the household, and if not, it would return to them.

If people reject us, there's nothing we can do about it. Our presence in their lives brings a test to them. Will they accept or reject the Word and the Spirit we bring? We just have to keep praying. We are not to fight against them. If our peace leaves them, they will feel it.

The Scripture says, "And stay in that house, eating and drinking what they give you; for the laborer is worthy of his wages. Do not keep moving from house to house" (Luke 10:7–8). This simply tells us to go and be where God sends us. I'd rather be where God tells me to be than where others want me to be.

HE SENT THEM TO BE REJECTED

THE MASTER INSTRUCTED the harvest workers to go to a city and eat what was set before them. They were to heal the sick and tell those in the city that God's kingdom was very near to them (Luke 10:8–9). That is our job as well—to go and bring peace to the houses we enter. Speak peace to our cities. Speak peace to our communities and proclaim that "the kingdom of God has come near you." The reason we can say that the kingdom of God has come near them is because the kingdom of God is within us.

If we enter a city in the name of the Lord by His command and the people do not receive us, we are told to go out into the streets and wipe the dust off our feet in protest (Luke 10:9–11). When people reject us as we come—in the name of the Lord, not in our own names—they reject the peace of the kingdom. They are already in condemnation because they are alienated from God. That condemnation will become very real to them if they reject the hour of their Holy Spirit visitation. Conviction and condemnation will come upon them. Our hearts should weep over this.

God extends to the world His hand of mercy, forgiveness and reconciliation through the cross of Jesus Christ. If people reject His gift, if they refuse His forgiveness and do not repent, eventually judgment and condemnation will come upon them. "The one who listens to you listens to Me, and the one who rejects you rejects Me; and he who rejects Me rejects the One who sent Me" (Luke 10:16).

When we are sent by God we become Christ's voice. We become His hands and His feet. We become His ambassadors. We become His representatives; this is why we need to be filled with His praises, peace, wisdom and strength. Wherever we go, we need to speak the oracles, or very words, of God. We have to speak as if God Himself were speaking through us, because we become His voice (1 Pet. 4:11).

When we develop a deeply intimate relationship with God, the Word and its principles will flow out from our relationship with Him to the world. It's not just our words that will bring life to others and turn them to the Lord. It is the power of the Holy Spirit that flows from our innermost beings through our words (2 Cor. 3:6).

HE SENT THEM DESIRING
THEY HAVE NO PREJUDICE

There came a woman of Samaria to draw water. Jesus said to her, "Give Me a drink." For His disciples had gone away into the city to buy food. The Samaritan woman therefore said to Him, "How is it that You, being a Jew, ask me for a drink since I am a Samaritan woman?" (For Jews have no dealings with Samaritans.)

Jesus answered and said to her, "If you knew the gift of God, and who it is who says to you, 'Give Me a drink,' you would have asked Him, and He would have given you living water." She said to Him, "Sir, You have nothing to draw with and the well is deep; where then do You get that living water? You are not greater than our father Jacob, are You, who gave us the well, and drank of it himself, and his sons, and his cattle?"

Jesus answered and said to her, "Everyone who drinks of this water will thirst again; but whoever drinks of the water that I shall give him shall never thirst; but the water that I shall give him shall become in him a well of water springing up to eternal life." The woman said to Him, "Sir, give me this water, so I will not be thirsty, nor come all the way here to draw. . . ."

At this point His disciples came, and they marveled that He had been speaking with a woman; yet no one said, "What do You seek?" or, "Why do You speak with her?" So the woman left her waterpot, and went into the city, and said to the men, "Come, see a man who told me all the things that I have done; this is not the

Christ, is it?" They went out of the city, and were coming to Him. . . .

"Do you not say, 'There are yet four months, and then comes the harvest'? Behold, I say to you, lift up your eyes, and look on the fields, that they are white for harvest. Already he who reaps is receiving wages, and is gathering fruit for life eternal; that he who sows and he who reaps may rejoice together. For in this case the saying is true, 'One sows and another reaps.' I sent you to reap that for which you have not labored, others have labored and you have entered into their labor."

—JOHN 4:7–15, 27–30, 35–38

This woman from Samaria was different. She desired to have a refreshing drink of water not only for her physical need but for her real need, which was to have a drink for her soul. Our prejudices hinder the thirsty from taking a drink of His pure water. It's evident that the disciples held some prejudices toward her. As we become more intimate with Jesus Christ, He rids us of our prejudice. Prejudice leaves when we fall in love with the Lord of the harvest. We start to love what He loves. He brings such love and healing to our hearts that it gets rid of our racism.

The disciples normally would not have spoken to a woman—especially a Samaritan woman. This woman was looked down upon. She came from a rejected group of people, an unacceptable group of people. She was of a mixed race and considered to be from a lower class.

When feelings of prejudice are removed from our hearts, it's a reflection of our intimate walk with God. If the prejudices remain, it indicates we aren't as intimate with God as we think we are. When we become like Jesus, we won't be afraid to be seen with people who are different from ourselves or who come from a different social status.

Jesus told the woman at the well that those who worship must do so in spirit and truth. He laid out for her who He was and how she was to worship. What's so exciting to me is that Jesus took the time to be with her, a rejected woman. He was no respecter of persons (Acts 10:34). This is what happens to us in our intimate walk. We start to appreciate every difference, every color, every social strata. We start to appreciate the young and the old, the black, brown, white, yellow and red. We start to celebrate God's beautiful diversity in the family of humanity.

When we start to appreciate the differences, we don't say, "I don't see color; I don't see the differences." The fact is when our eyes are opened like Jesus' eyes, we do see the differences. But we don't see them in the same way we saw them before. We see them with an eye of admiration. We admire what God has shaped and formed.

HE SENT THEM TO LOVE THE LOST

GOD IS NOT only concerned with what we do with our *outward actions,* but with our heart and our *inward attitudes* (Mark 2:8). He knows what goes on inside, but other people don't always. If we're going to go out to the harvest fields to be with the Samaritans, so to speak, we must be real and genuine in our love and respect toward them. Otherwise, they'll know we are fakes.

When the disciples asked Jesus to eat following the incident with the woman at the well, He responded in an unusual manner. "But He said to them, 'I have food to eat that you do not know about'" (John 4:32).

The disciples wondered if someone had brought Him some food. "Jesus said to them, 'My food is to do the will of Him who sent Me, and to accomplish His work'" (John 4:34). This is our food, too. It is to do the will of the Father and to do what He has called us to do, just as Jesus did.

The Samaritan woman didn't feel she could have the experience of discovering Christ without going out and telling others about Him. She went immediately to give her testimony to others. When we are an effective witness and "do the work of an evangelist," it's an indication of an intimate walk (2 Tim. 4:5–6). It's the fruit of an intimate walk. We become as Paul—a drink offering. When a person receives a burning desire to win souls for God, he or she experiences a very intimate knowledge of God's own heart.

We are fulfilled when our food is to do the will of Him who sent us and to accomplish His work. We receive a certain satisfaction. Accomplishing His will becomes our food, our sustenance.

Jesus was commending this Samaritan woman for returning to her village to share with many others. This new convert became an evangelist herself by going back and winning others.

HE SENT THEM TO POUR OUT
THEIR SOULS FOR OTHERS

JESUS HAD BEEN alone with the Father when He was able to come before His Father to share what was on the hearts of the lost. He had poured out His soul to the Father in prayer. If we're able to pour out our souls to the Lord and to one another, we'll have an even greater ability to allow others to pour out their souls to us. Because of the sensitivity we receive during our intimate times with the Holy Spirit, we will have great understanding when we speak to others.

Jesus is telling us today to lift up our eyes beyond our own self and needs. But we have to make an effort. There are certain things we have to do. He's saying, "Let your eyes be touched with eye salve, and let Me open them and show you what I see: the fields. They are white for harvest." (See Revelation 3:18.) Ask God to give you a vision. Ask God to reveal His heart to you and open up your eyes so you can see with His eyes. Already he who reaps is receiving wages and is gathering fruit for life eternal, so that he who sows and he who reaps may rejoice together (John 4:38).

HE SENT THEM OUT IN UNITY

IN THE TIME of harvest everyone does something. Some do one thing within the body of Christ, and some do another. But we're all going to benefit. Some come over and just help bring in the harvest but don't share in it. Others benefit from the harvest directly. I saw this in action at the harvest I witnessed. My friends and their livestock benefited directly. The man who had the tractor to cut and bale the hay shared in the harvest in a different way. He shared by taking half the crop home as payment for his labor. There was no exchange of money.

Others who didn't live on the land came to take part in the harvesting. I feel that this speaks to our churches. Many pastors and leaders are afraid to help another ministry because that ministry may have more people attend their church or become better known as a result. They don't want to see the success of another. They can't rejoice with another's success. Scripture says that when one weeps, the other weeps; when one hurts, the other one hurts (Rom. 12:15). We should all be partakers of the good things together. At the same time, when one is feeling rejection or sadness, we should all feel with that person. Sometimes we just need to be with that person and just be quiet in his or her presence.

The Lord is calling all of us to participate in the harvest. Some of us reap and some of us sow, but the Lord is the

One who gives the increase. He is the Lord of harvest. He is the One who brings the answers. There's no room for division. There's room only for unity. The Bible appeals to us as believers to come into unity. It's an appeal straight from the heart of God.

> Now I exhort you, brethren, by the name of our Lord Jesus Christ, that you all agree, and there be no divisions among you, but you be made complete in the same mind and in the same judgment. For I have been informed concerning you, my brethren, by Chloe's people, that there are quarrels among you. Now I mean this, that each one of you is saying, "I am of Paul," and "I of Apollos," and "I of Cephas," and "I of Christ." Has Christ been divided? Paul was not crucified for you, was he? Or were you baptized in the name of Paul? I thank God that I baptized none of you except Crispus and Gaius, so that no man should say you were baptized in my name.
>
> —1 CORINTHIANS 1:10–15

We are exhorted by Paul to be united as believers and to reject divisions. We have been sent like Paul to preach the gospel to the lost and needy souls on the earth. The Holy Spirit is moving upon believers everywhere, bringing us together in unity. When we yield to that holy move of the Spirit, we find there's little room left in our hearts for divisions. For far too long members of the church have feared the success of others and jealously fought to hold on to power and position. God is calling us to pull down religious pride and self-seeking. Labels dividing denominations must come off. We must take off pride, jealousy and privilege if we're going to take part in the great harvest of souls that awaits us.

I planted, Apollos watered, but God was causing the growth.

—1 CORINTHIANS 3:6

During this time of great ingathering of souls there will be no place for jealousy or competition. We hinder the harvest when we resist unity. We want to be better and bigger than the church down the street. But we are not growing bigger; we are getting in the way of God's divine plan. We are not operating from the mind of Christ.

For the harvest to come in, we must live lives that reflect John 3:30: "He must increase, but I must decrease." Jesus Christ must increase in us as individuals, and He must increase in us corporately as well. We must decrease to make a way for the harvest and for the Lord of the Harvest. We must be possessed by Christ and emptied of ourselves.

> And they came to John and said to him, "Rabbi, He who was with you beyond the Jordan, to whom you have borne witness, behold, He is baptizing, and all are coming to Him." John answered and said, "A man can receive nothing, unless it has been given him from heaven. You yourselves bear me witness, that I said, 'I am not the Christ,' but, 'I have been sent before Him.' He who has the bride is the bridegroom; but the friend of the bridegroom, who stands and hears him, rejoices greatly because of the bridegroom's voice. And so this joy of mine has been made full. He must increase, but I must decrease."
>
> —JOHN 3:26–30

We have often heard it said that to prepare the way for the Lord, we must take every hindrance out of the way. But too often the hindrance is us. We hinder the Lord's purpose and plan with our jealousy, self-seeking and pride.

REFLECTIONS OF THE GREAT HARVEST

TODAY I JOINED the harvest ingathering at my friends' farm. With more than five hundred bales of hay to gather, cut and store for the winter, it was important to gather the ripe hay quickly. So men and boys from many places joined in the work. Half of the hay was gathered in less than two hours.

One of the interesting things about today's harvest is that those who came to help were city folks. Only one out of the group of thirty men, women and children was a farmer. But everyone pitched in, taking a suitable part in the work at hand. Some served the others as they worked and prepared for the celebration afterward.

As I meditated on this wonderful event, I asked God to give me a living lesson from this day. I thought of the prophetic symbolism involved in the harvest.

Time after time prophets in our generation have declared that God intends to gather in a mighty harvest of souls. As I looked out over the fields, I thought about the many people God will bring into His kingdom—people of every kindred, tribe, tongue and nation being harvested into the house of God.

Long ago Jesus looked out over the fields and saw another harvest of His day: a harvest of souls. We must ask the Holy Spirit to show us what Jesus saw—and what He sees today as He looks at the earth. We must yield our hearts to a vision of souls ready and waiting to be saved and brought into the Father's house, where they can be healed and nurtured for eternity.

Another thing I noticed about today's harvesting is that although the workers were inexperienced, they did an excellent job—as well as they could do. The children discovered creative ways to help. One little boy had a wagon, and with it he carted a huge bale of hay to the barn. Another boy used a garden wheelbarrow, and he was able to bring in two bales of hay. The children were wonderfully ingenious and full of zeal. Two pickup trucks held more than thirty large bales, whereas the little wagon could only hold one. One bale of hay brought in by one little boy was just as important as all the bales brought in the big trucks driven by grown-up men.

Everyone rolled up their sleeves and pitched in, and the unity made for an exciting time. A celebration at the day's end capped off the completed work. Together the hungry harvesters shared a fine meal that several had prepared—a meal eaten in celebration of what God had done in His faithfulness.

This is what it's going to be like. As the harvest comes in, we'll rejoice together. Then we'll have a wonderful celebration and a big meal at the end of time when we meet our beloved Lord.

During dinner at the farm, we all fellowshiped and talked. Some of the people there had known each other for many years and attended the same church; some came from other churches that wanted to help. Even a few strangers came, having just met the others for the first time.

What a tremendous example of what God is doing in the body of Christ! He's bringing us together in unity. We're coming together to help those we've never met before. The unity I witnessed today was a beautiful thing—so many people helping. And the work was completed sooner than expected.

When the sky turned dark and the stars came out, someone lit a bonfire. As we sat together we shared a great sense of satisfaction and fulfillment. We reflected on our day, the day of the harvest, and we talked about God's grace. We experienced a sense of peace, rest and fulfillment, a sense of what it will be like when the Lord of the Harvest finishes His ingathering of souls.

I Love the Lord of the Harvest

Jesus said to them, "My food is to do the will of Him who sent Me, and to accomplish His work."

—JOHN 4:34

FULFILLING THE FATHER'S WILL
IS THE FRUIT OF INTIMACY

WE WORKED WELL and then ate well. Fulfilling the will of the Father is the fruit of intimacy with the Beloved. Bringing in the bales of hay was a prophetic act of the great harvest to come.

I thank the Lord for the opportunity to stay in the cottage on the farm to write part of this book. The Holy Spirit met me there in a special way. From the living room window of the cottage, I could look out over the fields to see they were ripe unto harvest. Many of us are looking out our windows. We see in our streets, communities and cities that the fields are ripe for harvest.

It is in our prayer closet that we begin to see the world through God's eyes. As we look through His eyes we will be filled with great vision, compassion and motivation. Afterward we will go out to help bring in the harvest of souls. This is the fruit of intimacy with the Beloved. We will gather in that harvest with the tools of wisdom and power that we've gained in our intimate moments with the Lord of the Harvest.

I learned so many things as I shared in the hay harvesting. I saw the answer to prayer in the natural, for my friends had prayed for workers for this great task. I saw a physical sign of what it is to have prayer answered after you beseech the Lord of the Harvest. As we pray in the closet and beseech the Lord, we experience the heart and compassion of God. But something more happens to us. When we come out of the closet, we are motivated to compel people to come in. (See Luke 14:23, NKJV.)

Many times we do not beseech the Lord before we run out

and try to compel others to come in. We must allow the Holy Spirit to reveal when the time is right to go out and win souls. To be successful, we must always be led of the Holy Spirit.

> And He also went on to say to the one who had invited Him, "When you give a luncheon or a dinner, do not invite your friends or your brothers or your relatives or rich neighbors, lest they also invite you in return, and repayment come to you. But when you give a reception, invite the poor, the crippled, the lame, the blind, and you will be blessed, since they do not have the means to repay you; for you will be repaid at the resurrection of the righteous."
>
> —LUKE 14:12–14

The Lord gave us careful instructions. He tells us the ones we should invite to our homes to have dinner with us. More than the kinds of people to whom we should go, the Lord is instructing us here about the kind of heart we should have as we go. We are not to look for anything in return. The Lord will reward us at the ingathering celebration.

PREPARATION FOR HARVEST

BEFORE THE HAY was brought in, my friend cleaned out his barn. This too is an exciting principle to me. The house of God has to be made ready. It has to be cleaned; it has to be purified. It needs to be in a state of repentance and holy living so that when God is ready to send in the harvest, the barn will be prepared. Our house will be clean.

The house of God needs to be ready to receive those who are new because we'll have to teach them, and what we give them must be pure. Therefore, we must walk in holiness and righteousness and be examples.

When the harvest came in, all the bales were stacked. The hay nearly reached up to the ceiling. God wants us to do this as well. God wants to fill our churches and our homes with people—with the saved who have been gathered in the harvest. We must be ready.

I received another revelation as I watched intercessors out there on the field with the workers. They encouraged the others. We go in the prayer closet to pray, but then we come out to encourage those for whom we pray.

Once you come into a place of intimacy with the Lord, being filled with His love and goodness, you find that you want to be positive. You want to encourage others, find out how they're doing and how you can help them. It's a blessed thing to encourage someone else or to lovingly assist them in their work. This is the fruit that comes from an intimate relationship with Jesus Christ in the closet of secret prayer.

CONCLUSION

WE CAN TAKE our prayers out of the prayer closet and into the world. This doesn't necessarily mean getting on our knees in the streets or having a big prayer rally where others can see us pray openly. Sometimes it will mean just being who we are—being a living prayer.

When we display the fruit of intimacy with God, we bring His presence to others—we bring that fragrance of Him from our prayers.

I believe the answer to the need for worldwide evangelism is passion for Christ. When we, His laborers, feel His heartbeat and know His passion, we will come to know what is in God's heart of hearts. The Lord loves people—and His heart is for the lost. When we experience true intimacy with Jesus Christ, we will love what He loves and seek what He seeks. Intimacy with Jesus is what motivates us to win the lost. Will we share Christ with people so that they can come to know the One who loves them?

I asked the Lord in prayer one day what was on His heart. He said, "People. People are on My heart."

I love the Lord of the harvest, therefore I love what He loves—and He loves the harvest!

NOTES

CHAPTER 3
A BRIDE WILLING TO PAY THE PRICE OF INTIMACY

1. J. I. Rodale, *The Synonym Finder* (Emmaus, PA: Warner Books, 1978).

CHAPTER 4
THE UNSEEN HAND

1. *Wycliffe Bible Encyclopedia*, Vol. 2 (Chicago, IL: The Moody Bible Institute of Chicago, 1975), 1471.
2. Ibid., 1025.

CHAPTER 8
LESSONS LEARNED FROM A CONSECRATED ONE

1. James Strong, *Strong's Exhaustive Concordance of the Bible* (Nashville, TN: Regal Publishers, Inc.), s.v. 6382. See also *The Hebrew Greek Key Study Bible, New American Standard Red Letter Edition* (Chattanooga, TN: AMG Publishers, 1990).

For additional information,
contact Rev. Pat Chen at:
First Love Ministries International
P.O. Box 1977
San Ramon, CA 94583-6977
Street Address: 12919 Alcosta Blvd, Suite 2A
San Ramon, CA 94583-1340
Phone: (925) 244-9600
Fax: (925) 244-9604

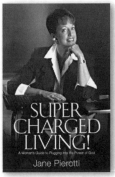